NEARLY NORMAL COOKING™ FOR GLUTEN-FREE EATING

by Jules E. D. Shepard

A portion of the profits from the sale of this book will be donated to the University of Maryland Center for Celiac Research.

ISBN 1-4196-4835-7
EAN13: 978-1-4196-4835-9

Interior formatting/design by
Rend Graphics
www.rendgraphics.com

Published by:
BookSurge Publishing, LLC.
5341 Dorchester Road
Suite 16
North Charleston, SC 29418

ACKNOWLEDGEMENTS

I could never have made it through the first few years of living gluten-free if it were not for my mother. She took on my disease as though it was her personal mission in life to keep my taste buds happy. Ultimately, it was her creation of my first recipe binder that set me on my way to finding a better way to cook gluten-free. Some of the recipes in this book are loosely based on these original recipes she gathered from everyone from personal friends to people she met at the health food store. I found it a challenge to try the recipes that sounded appealing and to improve upon them in my own ways. So I would be remiss if I failed to thank my mother as well as all those people out there who, whether they are aware or not, first provided their own recipe experiments to my mother, who then passed them on to me as inspirations for some of those you find in this book.

I also must thank my finicky husband as well as my pre-school son and toddler daughter who unknowingly taste-tested most of my creations. My husband's extreme distaste for most recipes utilizing rice flour caused me to re-examine the heavy reliance placed upon it by the majority of existing gluten-free cookbooks. My son has not yet learned that you never tell a cook you don't like her food, so together, they drove me to devise a better way to cook gluten-free. The results have won their approval, so I know they will win your family's too!

Finally, I must acknowledge the assistance of Dr. Alessio Fasano and the staff of the University of Maryland Center for Celiac Research. When I first found the Center, I had been bouncing around between various gastroenterologists, most of whom knew enough about celiac disease to be dangerous, but not to be particularly helpful. I felt like I was the only one in the world with this dining disability, and there was no one else who understood what I was going through. Everyone at the Center is excited about promising new research on celiac disease and is so supportive that their positive attitude is infectious. Without the help of Dr. Fasano, Maggie Burk and Pam Cureton, this book may not have become a reality.

Every man and woman is born into the world to do something unique and something distinctive and if he or she does not do it, it wll never be done.

-Benjamin E. Mays

Eating rice cakes is like chewing on a foam coffee cup, only less filling.

-Dave Barry

FOREWORD

By Alessio Fasano, M.D.
Medical Director, University of Maryland Center for Celiac Research
Professor of Pediatrics, University of Maryland School of Medicine
Director, Pediatric Gastroenterology & Nutrition, University of Maryland
Hospital for Children

Celiac disease (CD) is a condition characterized by damage of the small intestinal mucosa caused by certain proteins contained in grains such as wheat, barley and rye in genetically susceptible subjects. CD is one of the most common lifelong disorders in Europe and in the US. This condition can manifest with a previously unsuspected range of symptoms and at all ages, since it is now acknowledged that the disease may become clinically manifest after years of silent intestinal damage following exposure to gluten.

The keystone treatment of celiac disease patients remains a life-long elimination diet in which food products containing gluten are avoided. While in principle the treatment appears simple and straightforward, embracing a gluten-free diet is not an easy enterprise. There are things in life that we do automatically without paying attention to them. How many times do we drive back home from work thinking about something else and we find ourselves at the garage door without recalling how we got there? How often do we perform routine tasks such as tie our shoes, brush our teeth, listen to sounds of nature and yet, we don't have distinct memory of these acts? For the vast majority of human beings, eating is another automatic activity. Not for celiacs for whom eating is a very engaging task of their daily routine. A fair amount of mental, physical and social energy is devoted to what should be one of the most natural and enjoyable activities. In the U.S. this task has been aggravated in the past by the limited alternatives to gluten-containing food.

Jules experienced first-hand the journey from the dark times of the rice and banana diet to a more humane way of eating. With this book titled: *Nearly Normal Cooking™ for Gluten-Free Eating*, Jules is closing the gap between celiac and non-celiac cuisine to reach the holy grail of handing to the celiac community the pleasure of eating as a routine activity. Some of her recipes are based on those found in regular cookbooks, even if few people realize they can be served to people embracing a gluten-free diet. With this book, Jules offers both humor and help for others sharing in the gustatory limitation of CD.

INTRODUCTION

Let's face it. When you walked out of the doctor's office the day you were diagnosed with celiac disease or an allergy to wheat, you probably felt a confusing mixture of relief at finally knowing what in the world was wrong with you and dismay at learning that there was nothing left you could eat!

Gastroenterologists (God love 'em) exist to diagnose the cause of your distress, but then they usually send you out into the world alone to find some way of sustaining yourself sans gluten. Fortunately for your doctor, after delivering the news of your disease or allergy, he or she likely enjoyed a lunch comprised of *real* food, never stopping to read labels or worry about what might lurk in modified food starch. You, on the other hand, must learn to fend for yourself!

I first titled this cookbook "What to Cook When There's Nothing Left You Can Eat" because that is exactly the way that I felt for the first years after my own diagnosis with celiac disease, and it is exactly the way most celiacs have been forced to think about food. I settled on the "Nearly Normal Cooking™" title because many of the recipes contained in my book are indeed *real* food recipes that taste *really* good – offering a pleasant solution to this perpetual celiac problem. The remaining recipes call for my version of gluten-free flour which truly produces "nearly normal" results.

I hope that this compilation provides you with a light-hearted, yet useful perspective on living life without gluten but also offers you new recipe ideas that you are not afraid to make for your discriminating spouse, new neighbor or disapproving mother-in-law.

Since modern medicine estimates that 1 in every 133 people in the United States has celiac disease, one would think that the disease would at least receive the gustatory attention it statistically merits; however, that has not been the case to date. I have several complaints about the state of gluten-free cooking today, and I have tried to address these issues in this book.

The main gripe I have with existing gluten-free recipes and commercially available gluten-free mixes is that most of them taste, well, how should I put this ... um, bad. Yes, bad. Well, granted, some of them are decent when they are piping hot out of the oven, but don't even think about resurrecting them for the next day's lunch. One of the reasons for this fatal flaw is their heavy reliance upon rice flour. I have found rice flour to be gritty and distinctive (in a bad way) in any recipe when used in large quantities. Look at the mixes on your shelf right now, or thumb through any gluten-free cookbook you already own, and I think you'll begin to see the pattern. The flavor and texture it creates is a tell-tale sign that a dish is gluten-free.

Another ubiquitous problem with typical gluten-free recipes and mixes is that the end result is invariably a crumbly mess. We have learned the hard way that gluten holds most recipes together, and apparently so far celiac chefs haven't found a great gluten-free alternative.

My final pet peeve with gluten-free cookbooks, in particular, is that they are annoyingly cheerful about living in a world without gluten. It's not easy. It's not fun. It's not very yummy. Why can't we just cut through the façade and be honest about it? The first step is acknowledging the problem, right?

With all that in mind, I embarked upon devising a better way of cooking gluten-free. Ultimately, my experiments proved so successful that they had to be shared!

The linchpin to these recipes is my own alternative to the all purpose gluten-free flours on the market and found in contemporary cookbooks. Mixing a large quantity of this flour and keeping it on your shelf to add to many ordinary recipes calling for wheat flour will allow you to expand your own cooking even further, and it won't break the bank to have it on hand. My goal in creating this all purpose flour was to have it taste *normal* — to have ladies over for tea without them ever knowing the scones they were raving about were gluten-free. Many of the specialized gluten-free recipes in this book also use alternative means for holding the final product together so you don't wind up following your family around with a dustbuster while they sample your creations.

In this book, I have also included recipes for *real* food! Many are like recipes non-celiacs might have in their own cookbooks without realizing they could serve them to their gluten-free friends! How many times have you been invited over for dinner, but the host is afraid to cook for you? This is the cookbook for you *and* for your friends. They will be relieved and amazed to see recipes in a gluten-free cookbook which utilize ingredients they might actually already have on their own shelves. You, too will appreciate not having to hit an expensive specialty food market to buy ingredients for many of my recipes. It should be a refreshing change to have a cookbook on your shelf with recipes you can proudly serve to others and still lick the bowl yourself.

These recipes are taste-tested by celiac and non-celiac friends (thank you all!) who are still willing to try gluten-free experiments. Some recipes also come from others who have done their own experimenting and want to share their successes. The origins of some of these recipes are unknown, as they have been passed around and modified over time. I have streamlined the recipes as much as possible so that fewer odd ingredients and precious minutes are necessary to pull them off. I hope that you can build upon these recipes, modify and even feel free to send me suggestions so that we can all live a happier gustatory existence!

In an effort to make this book the handiest one on your kitchen shelf, I have also cross-referenced several selected ingredients in a separate ingredient index so that if you happen to have something extra like sour cream in your refrigerator, you can thumb through the index for recipes using sour cream — everything from coffee cake to sweet potato casserole. Lastly, I have provided an "Equivalent Measurements" page with some quick measurement references you may find useful in your cooking.

Don't forget to check my website, www.nearlynormalcooking.com, for more tips and new recipes! Happy cooking and happy eating "nearly normal" food!

WHAT IS CELIAC DISEASE?

To the uninitiated, celiac disease is a genetically inherited autoimmune disorder also known as gluten intolerance. Gluten is the protein which provides elasticity in foods made with the grains wheat, barley and rye – grains that celiacs must avoid. Oats used to be included in this hazardous grains list, but recent studies in Finland, among others, have suggested that celiacs can safely include wheat-free rolled oats in their diets without adverse effects.[1]

Because celiac disease is not a food allergy, but rather an autoimmune disorder like diabetes or rheumatoid arthritis, those afflicted with it must have both a genetic predisposition as well as the presence of an environmental factor to trigger its onset. For most autoimmune diseases, the triggers are not yet known; however, for celiac disease, we know that trigger is gluten. In response to exposure to this trigger, celiacs produce antibodies to attack the gluten, but the same antibodies also attack the intestine, causing damage to the villi lining the small intestine as well as potentially instigating a host of resulting illnesses.

---

[1] The American Dietetic Association has also now concluded that a gluten-free diet may include rolled oats if celiacs limit their consumption to approximately one-half cup of dry whole-grain rolled oats per day. The Association cautions that only those oat products tested and found to be free of contamination should be ingested by those on gluten-free diets. It should be noted that not all physicians agree that oats may be safely included in a gluten-free diet, so check with your own gastroenterologist before incorporating oats into your diet.

The vexing difference between gluten intolerance and food allergies is that gluten intolerance often takes much longer for symptoms to arise after exposure, thus making the link between ingesting the offending substance and the symptomatic complaints difficult to recognize. In fact, because of a general lack of awareness of the many ways it can manifest itself, celiac disease has taken an average of 10 – 12 years to diagnose in most patients. Fortunately, a preliminary diagnosis can now be made with a simple blood test to screen for the presence of specific gluten antibodies, although an endoscopic biopsy of the small intestine is necessary before a formal diagnosis can be made.

Celiac disease is currently thought to affect nearly 1 in every 133 Americans, or over 2 million people in America alone. Recent studies show that the presence of celiac disease in the United States is as frequent as it is in Europe, and that similar results were obtained in Africa, South America and Asia, where celiac disease had previously been considered a rare disorder. These studies have led Dr. Alessio Fasano, the internationally recognized medical director of the Center for Celiac Research, to dub the disease "one of the most frequent genetically-based diseases of humankind".

Despite its apparent prevalence, celiac disease remains shockingly under-diagnosed. In 2003, researchers projected that there were 2,115,954 Americans with celiac disease, yet there were only 40,000 diagnosed cases.

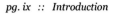

Thus, for each known celiac in the United States, there were 53 undiagnosed cases! It is now estimated that celiac disease is present in as many as one out of every 22 people who has first-degree relatives with the disorder, whether they manifest overt symptoms or not.

Researchers believe so many cases remain undiagnosed because celiac disease often presents itself in an atypical or even silent manner. Celiac symptoms fall into an unusually broad range of categories, including: gastrointestinal complaints such as irritable bowel syndrome, Crohn's Disease and ulcerative colitis; dermatological complaints like eczema, hives and acne; arthritic complaints including rheumatoid arthritis and possibly even fibromialgia; vitamin deficiencies; headaches and migraines; chronic fatigue; asthma, rhinitis or sinusitis; severe pre-menstrual syndrome; hypoglycaemia; depression; and sleeping disorders. Somewhat surprisingly, an even larger proportion of those with celiac disease may manifest no overt symptoms, though they face the same potential health consequences of the disease.

Thus, it is essential that diagnosis of gluten intolerance and avoidance of gluten by those with the disease be achieved at the earliest possible juncture. Research has shown that as little as ⅛ of a teaspoon of gluten (approximately 1/1,000 of a slice of bread) has a negative impact on the intestinal villi of a celiac patient. However, most physicians agree that with the proper diet, those suffering from celiac disease can enjoy a normal life expectancy and reduce or eliminate many varied physical complaints.

With that incentive in mind, let's get down to the business of making gluten-free cooking and eating as enjoyable as possible!

REFERENCES:

Agrawal, A., *Immunodominant Peptide Identified in Celiac Disease*, 2000 NAT. MED 6, at 337-342 (March 1, 2000), *available in* CELIAC.COM, "Diagnosis, Testing & Treatment of Celiac Disease: A Gluten-Free Diet" File.

Celiac Disease Not As Uncommon As Once Thought, Say Researchers At Wake Forest (Jan. 25, 2000), *available in* SCIENCE DAILY, Jan. 28, 2000 File.

Fasano, A., *Celiac Disease Finally Moves to Primetime in the United States*, MEDSCAPE (Oct. 14, 2003), *available in* WEBMD.

Fasano A, Berti I, Gerarduzzi T, et al., *Prevalence of Celiac Disease in At-Risk and Not-At-Risk Groups in the United States: A Large Multicenter Study*, 2003 ARCH. INT. MED. 163, at 286-292.

Fasano, A., *Celiac Disease: The Past, the Present and the Future*, 107 PEDIATRICS 4, at 768-770 (April 2001).

Farrell, R. and Kelly, C., *Celiac Sprue*, 346 NEW ENGL. J. MED. 180-188 (Jan. 17, 2002).

Gluten Intolerance No Longer Considered Rare, (Mayo Foundation for Medical Education and Research) Dec. 30, 2003.

Green, P.H. and Jabri, B., *Coeliac Disease*, 362 LANCET 9381, at 383-91 (Aug. 2, 2003), *available in* PUBMED.

Legislation is Passed Making Clearer Food Labels a Reality for Celiac Patients and Allergy Sufferers (*University of Maryland Medical News, Maryland*), July 21, 2004.

Nelson, D.A. Jr., *Gluten-Sensitive Enteropathy (Celiac Disease): More Common Than You Think*, 66 AM. FAM. PHYSICIAN 12, at 2259-66 (Dec. 15, 2002), *available in* PUBMED.

Oats and the Gluten-Free Diet, 103 J. AM. DIETETIC ASSOC. 3, at 376-79 (March 2003).

Oats Produce No Adverse Immunologic Effects in Patients with Celiac Disease, 2000 GUT 46, at 327-331 (Mar. 10, 2000), *available in* CELIAC.COM, "Diagnosis, Testing & Treatment of Celiac Disease: A Gluten-Free Diet" File.

Storsrud, S. et al., *Adult Coeliac Patients Do Tolerate Large Amounts of Oats*, 57 EURO. J. OF CLIN. NUTRITION 1, at 163-69 (Jan. 2003), *available in* NATURE.COM.

Thorn, M., *Celiac Disease: The Most Common Underdiagnosed Autoimmune Disease* (*Advance for Nurses*, Maryland/DC/Virginia), Jan. 17, 2005.

University of Maryland Study Shows Celiac Disease is More Prevalent in U.S. than Previously Thought (*University of Maryland Medical News, Maryland*), Feb. 10, 2003.

Westerberg, D. et al., *New Strategies for Diagnosis and Management of Celiac Disease*, 106 J. AM. OSTEOPATHIC ASSOC. 3, at 145-151 (Mar. 2006).

THE DO'S & DON'TS OF GLUTEN-FREE ("GF") LIVING

Although you should always check labels for other hidden sources of gluten, I have included a quick reference for grains and flours:

AVOID AT ALL COSTS:
- barley (including malt and malt flavoring)
- couscous
- oats, if contaminated with other gluten-containing grains
- rye
- triticale
- wheat in any form (including durum, semolina, kamut and spelt)

SAFE LIST:
- amaranth
- arrowroot
- bean (such as fava and garbanzo)
- buckwheat
- corn (starch, flour and meal)
- millet
- nut (such as almond)
- potato (starch and flour)
- quinoa
- rape seed oil (used to make canola)
- rice
- sorghum
- soy
- tapioca (starch and flour)

Unfortunately, a lot of packaged food companies haven't caught on to the gluten-free market yet, so you still must be vigilant when purchasing foods that tout the unusual flours found on your safe list. For example, a popular brand of packaged foods sold in many health food stores, "Health Valley," sells both Amaranth Crackers and Rice Bran Crackers. While theoretically both should be fine for folks with gluten sensitivity, only the Rice Bran Crackers are safe because the manufacturer has included whole wheat flour as well as amaranth in the other crackers. Incidentally, the rice bran crackers are akin to graham crackers and make s'mores possible again!

The magazine *Living Without (A Lifestyle Guide for People with Allergies and Food Sensitivities)* – a great resource for where to buy gluten-free foods and mixes, as well as for gluten-free recipes – sells packages of wallet-sized gluten-free guidelines if you have trouble keeping track of some of these obscure flours.

Gluten-Free Living and the online magazine *Celiac.com* also provide a wealth of resources for those eating gluten-free.

The passage of the Food Allergen Labeling and Consumer Protection Act of 2004 has made reading food labels far easier, as it requires food manufacturers to identify the top eight food allergens (including wheat) on all food labels. This same bill requires the Food and Drug Administration to issue final regulations by January 2008 defining "gluten-free". We can all look forward to future legislation specifically requiring food labels to reflect a gluten-free identifier as well.

MORE ON GRAINS

Grains will typically store well in cool, dry, airtight containers for about a year. If you are cooking with whole grains, you should first rinse them thoroughly to remove any dirt. Pour the cleaned grains into a heavy pot with a tight-fitting lid, add enough cold water to cover the grains and swirl the grains around in the pot with your hands. Pour them through a colander and return the grains to the pot, adding water and a pinch of sea salt. Cover and bring the water to a boil, then reduce the heat to simmer the grains, cooking covered until all the water is absorbed and the grains are soft.

Buckwheat:
Its name is somewhat of a misnomer, as it is from the rhubarb family (not from the wheat family) and is therefore safe for those with wheat and gluten sensitivities. It can be obtained in its natural form, roasted, un-roasted or as a flour.

Corn:
Corn is readily available as coarse or fine cornmeal (yellow or white), flour (masa flour), hominy or grits. Hominy is compromised of corn kernels that have been treated with lye and steamed, then hulled. Grits are coarsely ground and dried hominy.

Millet:
Millet has the distinction of containing more protein and iron than any other type of grain. It comes in its natural grain form, flakes or flour. If you purchase it as a grain, toast it before using it in your cooking by putting it in a large saucepan and stirring over a moderate heat for 3-4 minutes, or until it begins to have a roasted scent and some of the grains have popped. Remove from the heat and cool until ready to use.

Quinoa:
This grain is one of the oldest known varieties and it is very high in protein. It also has a distinctive nutty flavor. To cook raw quinoa, wash 1 cup of the grain thoroughly until the water is clear, then drain it well. It is important to wash quinoa well, as the grain has a natural coating that is quite bitter. Bring 3 ¾ cups of water to a rapid boil and add the cleaned quinoa. Cover and cook on low heat for 15 minutes. Remove from the heat and let stand for 5 more minutes. In this form, it can be used as a substitute for rice or salad and is good with vegetables and as a stuffing for peppers.

Rice:
Rice is available in its natural form, flakes, ground and as flour. As a raw grain, there are many different varieties, but they can be grouped into long-grain and short-grain types. In long-grain rice, the flavor is stronger and the grains separate when cooked, making them especially suitable for pilafs and rice salads. Short-grain varieties stick together and provide more fluffy texture. Brown rice is simply rice with only the inedible outer husk removed, while polished rice is completely white and lacking in many nutrients. Wild rice is even higher in protein than brown rice and has a smoky flavor. It is best cooked until it has absorbed all of the water in the pot: put one part rice into a saucepan with two parts water and a pinch of salt. Bring to a boil, then cover and reduce the heat to as low as possible until the water is fully absorbed by the grains.

BEER IS (NOT) GOOD FOR YOU!

Back in my college days I had a T-shirt with this affirmative mantra proudly displayed on the back, and on the front pocket it read something like, "Beer. It's Not Just for Breakfast Anymore." Unfortunately, we celiacs cannot enjoy beer at any meal of the day anymore, so we have been forced to find other alcoholic beverages to enjoy on social occasions.

There remains some controversy over the items in this categorization, but most agree that, based on their current ingredients, celiacs may safely partake in the following:

- Armagnac
- Brandy (those distilled from grapes or other fruits, such as Grand Marnier)
- Champagne
- Cider (those without barley additives)
- Cognac
- Gin
- Grappa
- Kahlua
- Meade
- Ouzo
- Rum
- Sherry
- Tequila (those containing 100% agave)
- Vermouth
- Vodka
- Whiskey
- Wine (including ports and sherries)

Notice that beer is not on this list, nor are typical wine coolers or hard lemonades and the like. Beer, of course, is made with grains celiacs must avoid (hence the wheat shaft pictured prominently on many beer labels) and most other bottled alcoholic beverages are made using malt (barley).

Unfortunately, manufacturers of alcoholic beverages rarely disclose exactly what goes into their product, so unless it is clearly displayed on the brand you wish to try, avoid it. A good rule of thumb is to stick with any alcohol which is distilled (including gin, rum, vodka and whiskey); the American Dietetic Association reported in 2000 that these alcohols are thereby rendered gluten-free.

As of the date of this publication, there are several folks trying hard to make and successfully distribute the elusive gluten-free beer. Recipes are on the internet and some breweries are already doing advance marketing. To date, there are at least three active gluten-free microbrews which are available in the United States, and Anheuser-Busch's new gluten-free label, "Redbridge," is available to every restaurant and store with a distributor for their beers. If your favorite establishments don't offer gluten-free beers yet, let your voice be heard! Ask them to request that their Anheuser-Busch distributor bring Redbridge on their next truckload and ... enjoy!

Nearly Normal Cooking™ for Gluten-Free Eating

ALL PURPOSE FLOUR

The recipes in this book which call for all purpose gluten-free flour contemplate a mixture that incorporates many different types of safe flours. This method reduces the distinctive taste and gritty texture of rice flour by cutting it with other milder starches and flours. The result is a versatile blend of flours that tastes – yes tastes – like the flour we all were raised on. I suggest preparing a batch or two of this all purpose blend by mixing it thoroughly in a large zippered plastic bag and keeping it in your cupboard or refrigerator at all times for use in your recipes. I won't guarantee that you can use it as a perfect substitute for wheat flour in every recipe, but it generally works quite nicely.

ALL PURPOSE NEARLY NORMAL GLUTEN-FREE FLOUR MIX™

1 cup white rice flour
1 cup potato starch
1 cup cornstarch
½ cup corn flour
½ cup tapioca flour
4 tsp. xanthan gum

OTHER TIPS

When rolling out cookies or doughs for pies, I suggest using cornstarch on your hands and on the rolling surface. Cornstarch will not leave behind any gritty texture or noticeable taste on your baked goods and it is always easy to find (and cheap!) in a grocery store. Non-stick rolling pins are also great tools for gluten-free doughs.

I have found that the airbake-type cookie sheets and muffin tins do not work well with gluten-free cooking. Your mom's good ol' fashioned cookie sheets and the new silicone muffin tins and bread pans seem to work best.

Try to make your baked goods, in particular, the day you want to serve them. Gluten-free foods always taste markedly better hot out of the oven. Also, gluten-free items often spoil sooner than those made with traditional ingredients. Freeze or refrigerate any portions you do not intend to eat that day, recognizing though, that this process tends to dry out breads and cakes.

Ingredients listed in this book, such as vanilla extract and baking powder, are intended to be of the gluten-free variety. Please ensure, for example, that you are using an aluminum-free baking powder such as Rumford brand, and that when you use a non-stick cooking spray, it does not also contain flour. When an oil substitute may be used, I recommend applesauce or a commercial variety such as Sunsweet's "Lighter Bake."

One last note about the recipes in the book. I receive emails all the time asking for substitutions to make my recipes dairy-free, egg-free, vegan, soy-free, low sugar, etc. To these requests, let me say that I am always happy to help you modify recipes to fit your individual dietary restrictions. With rare exception, recipes which call for butter can be made with vegan, dairy-free shortenings such as Earth Balance or Spectrum brand shortenings (also soy-free); soy vanilla yogurt can nearly always substitute for vanilla dairy yogurt; light and dark agave nectar work wonderfully as a substitute for honey or molasses (respectively); and Splenda, Stevia and other sugar substitutes can be used in most recipes as modifiers for granulated or brown sugars. Be sure to follow package directions on whatever substitute you are using to confirm proportions.

Starters, Salads & Soups

AUNT CONNIE'S DEVILED EGGS

If you knew my aunt Connie, you would know her famous deviled eggs. They are requested at every social gathering, and there are never enough.

6 hard boiled eggs
1 Tbs. mayonnaise
1 Tbs. mustard
1 Tbs. sugar
1 – 2 tsp. vinegar, to taste

Boil the eggs for 10 full minutes, cool, then peel under running water. Cut the eggs in half, lengthwise. Scoop out and mash the yolks in a small bowl. Mix in the other ingredients and stir until creamy. Scoop into the halved whites or use a disposable cake decorator with a wide tip. Refrigerate until serving.

Nearly Normal Cooking™ for Gluten-Free Eating

BAKED PINEAPPLE

This makes a nice side dish instead of applesauce, or it can be served over a meat, such as ham.

20 oz. can of crushed pineapple
2 Tbs. cornstarch
2 eggs, beaten
½ cup – 1 cup sugar
2 tsp. cinnamon

Preheat oven to 375 F.

Beat eggs until mixed and add drained pineapple. Stir together with cornstarch, cinnamon and sugar. You may add more or less sugar and cinnamon, according to your taste.

Pour into a greased 8 x 8 baking dish and sprinkle a dash of cinnamon on top. Bake for 25 – 30 minutes. This dish is especially good served warm.

BEEFY STEW

I go heavy on the vegetables in any soup or stew, so feel free to add more to this list to suit your own tastes. Depending on the season, try rutabagas, turnips or even green beans. Non-vegetarians tell me that the flavor of this stew is incredible, and the tapioca really helps as the thickening agent.

1 ½ lb. stew beef
1 onion
2 stalks celery, chopped
3 carrots, cut into ½ inch chunks
4-5 potatoes, peeled and cut into 1 inch chunks
2 tsp. garlic salt
¼ cup sugar
¼ cup quick cooking tapioca (in the box)
1 lg. can (28 oz.) tomato sauce

Preheat oven to 350 F.

Place beef and vegetables in a large oven-safe baking dish. Combine the rest of the ingredients and pour over the top. Cover and bake for 2 hours in the oven.

(Crock Pot cooking: low for 8 – 9 hrs. or high for 3 – 4 hrs.)

BLACK BEAN SOUP

This soup takes very little time to prepare and can be served on its own or over brown rice for extra fiber and protein. This soup is best if left to simmer for at least an hour before serving and is great the next day too.

2 16 oz. cans of black beans, rinsed and drained
4 cups vegetable broth
1 Tbs. red wine
1 Tbs. olive oil
1 cup chopped fresh onion or ½ cup chopped dried onion
½ cup chopped red, orange, yellow and/or green pepper
1 clove garlic, minced
½ tsp. black pepper
2 bay leaves
1 tsp. oregano
2 Tbs. chopped fresh or dried parsley
1 medium ripe tomato, chopped

In a large saucepan, heat oil over medium heat. Add the chopped onion and bell peppers, stirring until tender. Add the garlic and black pepper and cook for an additional minute. Add the broth, bay leaves and oregano and bring to a boil, increasing the heat if necessary. Reduce heat to low. Stir in the beans and simmer until the soup begins to thicken. Stir in the parsley, tomatoes and wine and remove the bay leaves shortly before serving.

CHEESE BALL OR SPREAD

Depending on your mood (or the time you have available), you can roll this spread in pecans and shape into a ball, or leave it in a bowl and serve it as a spread.

8 oz. cream cheese
1 – 2 Tbs. of gluten-free Ranch salad dressing
1 small jar of dried beef, chopped (optional)
1 – 2 green onions, chopped
salt and pepper to taste
chopped pecans (optional)

Bring cream cheese to room temperature to soften. Blend with chopped dried beef, green onions, ranch dressing, salt and pepper. Leave in the bowl or roll in pecans. Chill in the refrigerator for 1-2 hours.

Serve with celery sticks, gluten-free crackers or corn chips.

Nearly Normal Cooking™ for Gluten-Free Eating

CHRISTMAS LIME GELATIN SALAD

Not only is this salad appealing for all ages, it offers a festive green and red presentation for your holiday table.

1 small package (.3 oz) of lime gelatin
1 cup hot water
1 can crushed pineapple, drained
¾ cup pineapple juice (saved from the can)
1 large package cream cheese (cut into very small chunks)
½ pint whipped cream
chopped nuts and maraschino cherries, if desired

Combine gelatin, hot water and pineapple juice and chill until the mixture is almost firm. Add the crushed pineapple, chunks of cream cheese, whipped cream and nuts and cherries. Stir until blended and pour into a mold or square baking pan. Refrigerate until set.

CRANBERRY-PINEAPPLE SALAD

This easy and festive treat is almost too pretty to eat — but you will want to!

1 can (20 oz.) crushed, undrained pineapple
2 small packages (.3 oz each) of raspberry flavored gelatin
1 can (16 oz.) whole berry cranberry sauce
1 medium apple, chopped
2/3 cup chopped walnuts or pecans

Drain the pineapple but reserve the liquid in a 1 quart measuring cup. Remove
1 Tbs. of the crushed pineapple and set aside as garnish. Add enough cold water to
the juice to equal 3 cups total liquid and pour into a large saucepan. Bring to a boil,
then remove from heat. Add the gelatin and stir 2 minutes, or until it is completely
dissolved. Add the cranberry sauce and stir until well-blended. Pour into a large
bowl and refrigerate 1 ½ hours or until thickened to the consistency of egg whites.

Stir in the remaining pineapple, apple and walnuts, mixing gently until well blended.
Pour into a medium-sized serving bowl.

Refrigerate 4 hours more, or until firm. Garnish with reserved pineapple and
additional apple slices or cranberries, if desired, before serving.

Nearly Normal Cooking™ for Gluten-Free Eating

CRANBERRY SALAD I

This recipe comes down from my grandmother and always gets me in the mood for the holidays! It has a wonderful tart taste and substantial chunky texture.

2 oranges
1 lb. cranberries
2 cups sugar
1 medium can crushed pineapple, drained
3 small packages (.3 oz each) of cherry gelatin
2 ½ cups boiling water (over gelatin)
2 ½ cups boiling water (over sugar)
chopped nuts if desired

Mix sugar and water in one bowl and gelatin and water in another. Stir well until totally dissolved. Mix together in either one 9 x 13 pan or two square pans and refrigerate until it begins to thicken. Chop cranberries and oranges alternately in food processor. Add pineapple then add all fruit and nuts to gelatin/sugar/water mixture. Stir a couple more times as it is setting up to keep the fruit distributed. Chill until completely set.

May be served plain or with mayonnaise or whipped cream.

CRANBERRY SALAD II

This cranberry salad recipe comes from my other grandmother who found the original salad to be too tart for her tastes. In my family, we believe adding strawberries to just about everything makes it taste better!

.3 oz package of strawberry gelatin
1 cup boiling water
½ cup sugar
1 cup chopped cranberries
1 cup crushed pineapple, drained
1 large box sliced frozen strawberries, thawed and drained
1 cup chopped pecans

Mix together gelatin, sugar and water. Add cranberries to gelatin mixture and let stand about 30 minutes. Add pineapple, strawberries and pecans. Spray a 6 cup mold with non-stick cooking spray, pour in mixture and chill overnight.

Nearly Normal Cooking™ for Gluten-Free Eating

JAPANESE SALAD

This is one of those salads that is satisfying enough for a meal. Any meat will do here, but I have suggested chicken.

Salad:
1 – 1 ½ heads iceberg lettuce
3 – 4 scallions, chopped (green and white portions)
About ½ of 5 oz. can of gluten-free chow mein noodles
2 – 3 heaping Tbs. poppy seeds
sliced almonds (¾ – 1 cup)
2 grilled chicken breast(s), sliced (optional)

Dressing:
4 Tbs. sugar
4 Tbs. vinegar
3 tsp. seasoned salt
1 tsp. salt
½ tsp. pepper
½ cup vegetable/salad oil

Make dressing by combining all ingredients. Warm slightly in a saucepan over the stove or in the microwave just until sugar is melted. Meanwhile, tear lettuce into a serving bowl. Add chopped scallions and sliced chicken breasts. Add warmed dressing and toss. Lastly, add noodles, poppy seeds and almonds. Toss again slightly before serving.

HEARTY POTATO SOUP

This recipe comes from my grandmother, via my own mother — together, they have perfected this gluten-free comfort food.

6 – 8 medium white potatoes
1 onion, chopped
1 stalk of celery, chopped, or celery seed to taste
milk
¼ cup margarine or butter
salt and pepper, to taste

Peel, slice and cube the potatoes into small pieces. Place in large pan with water covering potatoes by about an inch. Add some salt to taste. Add the chopped onion and celery or celery seed. Cook until potatoes are tender. Drain off most of the water from the vegetables. Add enough milk to make the soup the amount and/or consistency you want. Begin heating the soup again and add the butter or margarine when it is hot. Do not boil! Add more salt and pepper, if desired.

This soup tastes even better after several hours and reheating.

HONEY NUT CHEESE WITH FRUIT

When you're looking for a quick appetizer to bring to a party — one that everyone will love and no one will think is easy — try this wonderful cheese dish.

8 oz. round of Brie or Camembert cheese (hint: Camembert is milder)
¼ cup butter or margarine
1 cup coarsely chopped walnuts, pecans, almonds or your favorite nut
½ tsp. ground cinnamon
¼ tsp. ground nutmeg
2 Tbs. honey
2 large apples, cored and thinly sliced
green or red seedless grapes

Melt butter in a 10-inch non-stick skillet and stir in the nuts and spices. Add honey and cook, stirring constantly until bubbly. Immediately pour over the cheese round. Heat apples in microwave or in skillet until warm and arrange around the cheese with grapes.

HOT ARTICHOKE DIP

This recipe is a favorite at parties and can be easily doubled. If doubling the recipe, put into two pie pans or one larger casserole dish.

1 can (14 oz.) artichoke hearts, drained and smashed
1 cup Miracle Whip salad dressing or mayonnaise
1 cup grated Parmesan cheese
minced garlic or garlic powder, to taste

Preheat oven to 350 F.

Mix all the ingredients together and spoon into a 9 - inch pie pan. Bake for 45 minutes, or until the top is lightly browned. Sprinkle with sliced green onions and chopped tomato, if desired. Serve with tortilla chips or gluten-free crackers.

SPINACH ARTICHOKE DIP

Stir 1 package (10 oz.) frozen spinach (thawed and well drained) into artichoke mixture. Bake as directed above.

Nearly Normal Cooking™ for Gluten-Free Eating

MANGO SALSA

This salsa is great with chips as an appetizer or over fish or chicken for a main dish. You may substitute cantaloupe, peaches or nectarines for the mango, but with any of these fruits, make sure that they are very ripe when you use them.

1 fresh, ripe mango, diced
½ cup diced red pepper
¼ cup diced red onion
½ tsp. cumin
¼ tsp. Tabasco sauce
1 Tbs. fresh lime juice (optional)
1 tsp. fresh, chopped cilantro leaves (optional)

Mix all ingredients in a bowl, cover and refrigerate until ready to serve.

Recipe Tip: Make sure to double the recipe if you are serving this as a salsa with corn chips at a dinner party because this dish is a huge hit!

MARYLAND CRAB BALLS

The Old Bay seasoning is a must to make these mini-crab cakes worthy of the "Maryland" moniker. You won't even miss the bread crumbs — I promise! If you prefer, this same recipe can be modified to make crabcakes.

1 lb. (16 oz.) lump crabmeat
1/3 cup minced green onions
1/3 cup chopped fresh parsley
2 Tbs. lemon juice
1 Tbs. milk
1 tsp. Tobasco sauce
1/2 tsp. salt
1/4 tsp. pepper
4 eggs
Old Bay seasoning to taste (the more the better!)
1/4 - 1/2 cup crushed corn tortilla chips (approximately)

1/2 cup crushed corn tortilla chips (for crab balls)
Gluten-free crackers
4 Romaine lettuce leaves

Combine first 10 ingredients and mix well. Add only enough crushed tortilla chips to hold the meat mixture together. Divide crabmeat into 16 equal portions if making crab balls, or 8 equal portions if making crabcakes. If making crab balls, dredge through crushed corn tortilla chips. Shape into balls or patties. Sprinkle tops with Old Bay seasoning.

To Fry: Heat olive oil over medium-high heat in a large skillet. Place balls or patties in hot oil and cook for 3 minutes on each side.

To Grill: Wrap each crab ball or crabcake in aluminum foil and grill for approximately 5 minutes per side.

To Broil: Place crabcakes on a greased baking sheet and broil for approximately 10 minutes, turning once.

Serve crab balls on gluten-free crackers with a small piece of lettuce under each ball. Serve crab cakes as a main dish or as an appetizer over lettuce.

Nearly Normal Cooking™ for Gluten-Free Eating

MEXICAN DIP

This version of the ever-popular layered bean dip comes from a friend whose family affectionately calls this "Bloat Dip," because it's so good that you always eat too much! It may be made one day ahead if covered and kept refrigerated, then baked just before serving.

1 Tbs. vegetable oil
1 ½ lbs. ground beef, shredded chicken or firm tofu, cut into chunks
1 ½ lg. onions, chopped
Salt and pepper
16 oz. can refried beans
7 oz. can diced green chilies, drained
1 cup salsa (or more)
2 cups shredded Cheddar cheese

Sour cream (optional)
Green onions, chopped for garnish (optional)
Tortilla chips

Preheat oven to 350 F.

Heat oil in heavy, large skillet over medium heat. Add meat or tofu and onions and cook until browned (about 5 minutes). Drain. Season with salt and pepper. Spoon half of beans into a 9 x 13-inch glass baking dish. Top with half of the meat mixture, followed by half of the chilies, half of the salsa and half of the Cheddar cheese. Repeat with remaining beans, meat, chilies, salsa and cheese.

Bake until heated through and cheese melts, about 30 minutes, or longer if using a smaller pan. Top with garnishes and serve warm with tortilla chips.

MOCK GUAC

If you love guacamole, but can actually feel it hit your thighs every time you eat it, try this variation and lose the guilt.

2 cups frozen asparagus, thawed
½ of a medium ripe avocado, peeled, pitted and chopped
3 ripe plum tomatoes, chopped and seeded
1 small red onion, chopped
¼ cup red pepper, chopped
3 Tbs. Ricotta cheese (may use fat free)
3 Tbs. lemon juice
¼ tsp. sea salt
⅛ tsp. cayenne pepper
Fresh cilantro, to taste
Corn tortilla chips

Place the thawed asparagus in a food processor or blender and blend until it is smooth. Combine the puréed asparagus, chopped avocado, Ricotta cheese, lemon juice, salt and cayenne pepper. Add the tomatoes, onion and red pepper to the avocado mixture. Scoop into a serving bowl and cover tightly. Refrigerate until you are ready to serve.

Garnish with cilantro and serve with corn tortilla chips.

Nearly Normal Cooking™ for Gluten-Free Eating

MOZZARELLA & TOMATO SALAD

Buffalo Mozzarella really makes this salad special, but in a pinch, you could use high quality Mozzarella slices. I was first introduced to the amazing flavor of fresh basil and Mozzarella while in Tuscany, where my husband and I routinely stopped at roadside stands just to eat Buffalo Mozzarella! If only we had such "fast food" here in the States!

3 medium-sized ripe tomatoes, peeled and sliced
1 round of Buffalo Mozzarella, or 16 oz. of sliced Mozzarella
Fresh basil leaves

Dressing:
½ cup canned crushed tomatoes
3 Tbs. Gluten-free balsamic vinegar or red-wine vinegar
1 tsp. thyme
½ tsp. Dijon mustard
¼ tsp. freshly ground black pepper

Place the tomatoes in a microwave-safe dish and microwave on high for 1 minute. The peels will then slip off. Slice the tomatoes thickly and arrange on individual serving plates. Slice the Mozzarella and arrange slightly askew over the tomatoes, one slice for every slice of tomato. Mix the dressing ingredients together and spoon over the tomatoes and cheese. Place one large leaf of fresh basil on top.

Note: An alternative to this dish is just to drizzle gluten-free balsamic vinegar or red-wine vinegar over the tomatoes and cheese and top with fresh basil leaves.

NEW PARTY MIX

I grew up munching on my mother's homemade party mix while watching football games and parades in the fall. This one is a variation on the old "chex mix," and it is a really tasty alternative. Try caramelizing the pecans and serving them on their own as an extra treat.

2 lb jar of salted cashews
14 oz. bag of gluten-free pretzels
1 large bag of halved pecans
¼ cup butter or margarine
⅛ cup sugar

Lightly brown pecans in a skillet with melted butter. Add sugar, stirring until the sugar is dissolved and the pecans are slightly shiny. Pour pecans onto a cookie sheet lined with paper towels. Spread the pecans over the paper towels, pat, then pour onto another unlined cookie sheet to cool. Add all cooled ingredients together in a large bowl and serve.

*BAKING TIP: For any recipe calling for draining fried foods onto paper towels, make sure to use a high-quality paper towel, such as Viva, so that the towels don't rip apart and stick to your foods!

PUMPKIN DIP

When I first tried this dip, I couldn't get away from it. It is not too sweet, and paired with even commercially available gluten-free gingersnaps, it is addicting! The recipe is extremely forgiving, so feel free to adjust the amounts of these ingredients to suit your own taste.

1 small can of pumpkin purée
8 oz. package of cream cheese (room temperature)
2 tsp. cinnamon
1 tsp. pumpkin pie spice
½ container of whipped topping (optional)
⅓ cup sugar

Mix all ingredients together until smooth and refrigerate. Serve with gluten-free gingersnaps for dipping.

SHRIMP DIP

This recipe is another easy, yummy option for parties.

¾ cup mayonnaise
¼ cup milk
8 oz. pkg. cream cheese
2 regular size cans shrimp, drained
¼ cup chopped onion
dash of paprika

Blend mayonnaise and milk until smooth. Add the remaining ingredients and refrigerate for at least 4 hours (overnight is best). Dip with potato chips, corn chips or gluten-free crackers.

Nearly Normal Cooking™ for Gluten-Free Eating

SPICY SEAFOOD SOUP

You may substitute mussels or scallops, to taste. This recipe is also delicious served over rice, paella-style.

¼ cup olive oil
5 garlic cloves, minced
1 bay leaf
1 tsp. dried crushed red pepper
1 cup dry white wine
1 (28 – ounce) can diced tomatoes
24 small Littleneck clams (about 2 ½ pounds total), scrubbed
24 mussels (about 1 ½ lbs. total), debearded
20 large shrimp (about 1 lb.), peeled, deveined and butterflied
½ cup torn fresh basil leaves
Gluten-free bread or breadsticks (see pg. 82)

Heat the oil in a heavy large pot over medium heat. Add the garlic, bay leaf and crushed red pepper. Sauté until the garlic is tender, about 1 minute. Add the wine and bring to a boil. Add the tomatoes and reduce to a simmer. Simmer until the tomatoes begin to break down and the flavors blend, about 5 minutes. Stir in the clams. Cover and cook for 5 minutes. Stir in the mussels. Cover and cook until the clams and mussels open, about 5 minutes longer.

Using tongs, transfer the opened shellfish to serving bowls (discard any shellfish that do not open). Add the shrimp and basil to the simmering tomato broth. Simmer until the shrimp are just cooked through, about 1 ½ minutes. Divide the shrimp and tomato broth among the bowls and serve with the warm bread gluten-free bread or breadsticks, for dipping.

SPINACH DIP WITH A KICK

This recipe has that southern spicy flair that makes it an out-of-the-ordinary dip. The secret is in the chilis and the Tobasco — it is a real crowd pleaser!

8 oz. cream cheese (light works fine too)
2 cups shredded Monterrey Jack cheese
1 can chopped chilis, drained
1 can chopped tomatoes, drained
2 block packages of frozen spinach
1 cup half and half or whipping cream
Tobasco sauce, to taste
½ cup grated Parmesan cheese

Preheat oven to 350 F.

Rinse the spinach until it is thawed and broken apart. Add it with all the remaining ingredients except Tobasco and Parmesan in a large bowl and mix well with an electric mixer. Add splashes of Tobasco sauce until it suits your taste. Pour into a greased oblong baking dish, sprinkle with Parmesan and bake for 10 minutes, or until the cheese has melted and the top is lightly browned.

Serve with corn tortilla chips.

Nearly Normal Cooking™ for Gluten-Free Eating

STRAWBERRY SOUP

This surprising mixture is one of our family's favorite North Carolina summer beach recipes. You must try it to believe how wonderfully well the ingredients come together into a refreshing appetizer or brunch offering.

2 pints fresh strawberries
½ cup sugar
¾ cup sour cream
½ cup half and half
1 ½ cups dry white wine
strawberries for garnish

Purée strawberries and sugar in a blender or food processor. Pour into a large bowl and whisk in sour cream, half and half and wine. Mix well and chill thoroughly. Serve in chilled glasses with strawberry garnish.

SWEET MUSTARD SHRIMP

This recipe is handy for entertaining, as the dressing may be made up to a week in advance and the entire dish may be prepared the night before.

½ cup dijon mustard
2 tsp. dried mustard
1 tsp. mustard seed, toasted
1 Tbs. fresh lemon juice
6 Tbs. sugar
½ cup apple cider vinegar

½ cup vegetable oil
1 tsp. ground cinnamon
2 Tbs. dried dill
2 Tbs. red onion, finely chopped
2 lbs. medium shrimp, cooked

Toast mustard seed on cookie sheet under a broiler for 1-2 minutes (until it starts popping like popcorn). Combine ingredients one through six and whisk in oil. Stir in cinnamon, dill and onion. Chill in a jar (keeps for about a week). Mix shrimp with dressing. Refrigerate at least 2 hours.

TACO DIP

1 lb. – 1.5 lb. ground beef or tofu
1 pkg. commercial taco seasoning (gluten-free)
1 can refried beans
8 oz. cream cheese
8 oz. sour cream
8 oz. shredded Cheddar cheese

Brown the beef or tofu and add the seasoning packet, cooking according to the package directions. Add in the beans and spread in the bottom of a casserole dish. In a separate bowl, mix the cream cheese and sour cream. Spread this mixture over the bean and meat mixture. Top with shredded cheese and bake for 30 minutes.

Serve with corn chips or place on a bed of greens with tomatoes.

WHITE CHILI

On a cold day, this low-fat, satisfying chili is great for the whole family. You may reduce the amount of green chilies to bring down the spicy flavor. It is fabulous with some gluten-free corn bread (pg. 96) or with the Okra Griddle Cakes (pg. 37) and is great for left-overs the next day.

1 lb. Great Northern beans or Cannellini beans, soaked (or canned)
1 med. onion, chopped
3 cloves garlic, minced
4 oz. can green chilies
2 tsp. cumin
1 tsp. oregano
1 ½ tsp. cayenne pepper
½ tsp. salt
2 ½ cups vegetable broth
2 lbs. chicken breast, cut into 1 in. cubes (optional)

Add all ingredients to crock pot. Stir well. Cover and cook on low (10 hrs.) or high (5 hrs.).

You can also simmer on the stove top for 2 hours until the flavors are well blended.

Veggie Sides

ASPARAGUS CASSEROLE

A Thanksgiving favorite in my family, I modified this recipe as soon as I was diagnosed with celiac disease because sometimes, you just need this wonderful side dish! I even keep a brick of Velveeta cheese in my refrigerator just for this recipe.

1 can asparagus spears
        (or enough fresh steamed asparagus to thickly cover your casserole dish)
2 ½ Tbs. butter or margarine
1+ cups potato chips*
1 ½ Tbs. Nearly Normal Gluten-Free Flour Mix™
¼ - ½ cup milk
1 ½ thick Velveeta cheese slices, to your taste

Preheat oven to 350 F.

Melt 1 Tbs. butter into an 8 x 8 casserole. Add ¾ cup crushed potato chips. Arrange asparagus spears on top of the chips.

Make a roux of 1 ½ Tbs. of melted butter and 1 ½ Tbs. Nearly Normal Gluten-Free Flour Mix™ by stirring over low heat until thickened. Slowly add ¼ - ½ cup of milk and thin with asparagus juice until it is the consistency of thick milk. Add 1 ½ thick slices of Velveeta cheese and melt together in the unique way that only processed orange-colored cheese can melt. Pour roux over the asparagus and sprinkle with remaining chips.

Bake for 20 – 25 minutes.

*BAKING TIP: If you are using regular potato chips, do not melt any butter, simply put the crushed chips into the bottom of the pan and sprinkle plain chips on top of the casserole. If you are using the baked variety of potato chips, however, add the butter as directed.

FAUXTATOES
(a.k.a. Mashed Cauliflower)

I am not personally a big fan of cauliflower, so any recipe that makes cauliflower taste like potatoes is a winner in my book.

1 head of cauliflower
3 – 4 Tbs. butter or margarine
½ cup half & half (fat free works fine too)
½ – ¾ cup Parmesan cheese, to taste
1 small shallot or ¼ cup scallions, chopped (optional)
Salt and pepper to taste

Cut up the cauliflower into small pieces and steam just until tender. Drain cauliflower, emptying the water from pan and returning the cauliflower to the pan. Cook over medium heat until the cauliflower is of a consistency that could mimic a cooked potato. Remove from heat and allow to cool slightly. Drain to remove as much moisture as possible.

Put cooled cauliflower into a food processor with the steel blade and process with pulse button several times. Add half of the cream and all of the cheese and process until smooth. If it is too dry, add the remaining cream until the cauliflower is the consistency you prefer for mashed potatoes. Add salt and pepper to taste and toss in the shallots or scallions before serving.

*As a variation, you can include a small can of drained mushrooms (stems and pieces are fine) at the same time you add the shallots or scallions.

FRIED ZUCCHINI

This is an old family recipe passed down orally through the generations. It is a great way to get kids (or green vegetable-fearing adults) to eat zucchini!

1 large zucchini
2 cups corn meal
¾ cup sugar
2 eggs, beaten
Vegetable or Canola oil

Prepare two bowls, one with the beaten eggs and one with a mixture of the corn meal and sugar.

Slice the zucchini thinly and dip each slice first into the eggs, then into the corn meal mixture. Place each dipped slice into a frying pan with hot oil. Fry each side until lightly browned, then turn. Place each fried slice onto a cookie sheet lined with crumpled paper towels* and place full cookie sheet in a warm oven to keep crisp and hot until ready to serve.

*BAKING TIP: For any recipe calling for draining fried foods onto paper towels, make sure to use a high-quality paper towel, such as Viva, so that the towels don't rip apart and stick to your foods!

Nearly Normal Cooking™ for Gluten-Free Eating

GINGER EGGPLANT

You've probably already discovered the benefits of ginger in your diet – I try to use it wherever I can when cooking. A gourmet friend of mine in North Carolina (who has more patience in the kitchen than I have) sent me a yummy, but even more complicated version of this recipe. I've pared it down to the bare essentials, but please don't skimp on the fresh ginger!

1½ pounds eggplant, ends trimmed and
    cut lengthwise into ½-inch thick slices
1 tsp. salt
2 tsp. minced garlic
1½ cups chicken or vegetable broth
1½ Tbs. rice wine or sake
1 Tbs. sugar
1 Tbs. vegetable oil

1½ tsp. hot chile paste or oil
1½ tsp. hot chile paste or oil
1½ Tbs. minced fresh ginger
2½ Tbs. gluten-free soy sauce
1 Tbs. Worcestershire sauce
1 Tbs. cornstarch
2 cups onion — coarsely chopped
1 medium red pepper, cored, seeded
    and coarsely chopped

Arrange eggplant slices on a cookie sheet lined with paper towels. Sprinkle both sides with salt and let them sit 1 hour, then pat them dry. Cut the salted eggplant into strips about ½ inch thick and about ½ inch long.

Mix the chile paste, garlic and ginger in a bowl. Separately mix the broth, soy sauce, rice wine, Worcestershire sauce, sugar and cornstarch.

Heat a large pan on the stove top. Add oil and when heated, add the chile paste mixture, stir-frying over medium heat until fragrant. Add the onions and sauté about 1 ½ minutes, then add the red pepper and sauté another minute. Add the eggplant cubes and stir-fry for 2 to 3 minutes. Next add the liquid mixture, cover and heat until boiling. Reduce the heat to medium, cover and cook about 12 to 15 minutes, or until the eggplant is tender. Uncover, return the heat to high and cook until the sauce is reduced.

GREEK MASHED POTATOES

Ok, so this recipe didn't really come from Greece, but it could have! I use feta cheese to liven up mashed potatoes, but you could use just about any kind of soft gluten-free cheese you have on hand.

3 average sized baking potatoes, peeled and cut into approximately 2 inch chunks
Sea salt & coarsely ground pepper, to taste
1 cup milk
4 oz. feta or other soft cheese
2 thinly sliced scallions, leeks or shallots, depending on your taste preference

Mix the potato chunks, a dash of salt and enough cold water to measure 2 inches deep in a large saucepan. Boil over medium to high heat. Reduce to medium-low heat and simmer for approximately 15 minutes, or until the potatoes are tender but not mushy.

Drain the potatoes and return them to the saucepan. Cook over medium-low heat while adding the milk and feta cheese. Mash the mixture together using a potato masher until it is the consistency you prefer for mashed potatoes. Season with salt and pepper and stir in the scallions, leeks or shallots. Serve warm.

HASH BROWN CASSEROLE

This is wonderful recipe that even my picky toddler loves to eat. It is very forgiving too, so feel free to add or subtract ingredients to fit what you have on hand.

8 oz. sour cream (light sour cream works fine too) or plain yogurt
8 oz. shredded Cheddar cheese
1 can gluten-free cream of mushroom soup (Progresso brand is currently gluten-free)
2 lb. frozen shredded hash brown potatoes, thawed
½ cup frozen or fresh chopped onion
½ – 1 cup crushed baked potato chips

Preheat oven to 350 F.

Grease a large oblong casserole dish and set aside.

In a large bowl, stir together the sour cream, cheese, soup and onions. Add the hash browns and mix together well. Spread the mixture into the casserole dish and top with the crushed baked potato chips.

Bake for at least 1 hour, until the chips are lightly browned and the cheese is bubbly.

MILLET PILAF

This pilaf makes a sweet and nutty change to traditional rice pilaf and has the added benefit of being especially high in protein and iron.

1 ½ cups millet
1 Tbs. oil
1 small onion, peeled and chopped
2 large carrots, peeled and diced
1 clove garlic, crushed (or, for milder flavor, use jarred garlic or garlic powder)
1 piece of fresh ginger, grated
1 stick of cinnamon
3 cups water
pinch of salt and pepper
⅓ cup raisins (optional)
½ cup almonds, slivered and toasted (optional)

Toast the millet by placing it in a large saucepan and stirring it over medium heat for about 3 or 4 minutes, or until some of the grains begin to pop. Remove from heat.

Heat the oil in another saucepan and sauté the chopped onion until clear. Add the carrots, garlic, ginger and cinnamon at this point and cook for 5 minutes.

Add the toasted millet to the saucepan mixture and pour in the water. Season to taste with salt and pepper.

Bring to a boil, then cover and turn the heat down to low, cooking for 15-20 minutes, or until the water is absorbed and the millet is tender.

Add the raisins and almonds at this point, if you desire, by mixing in lightly with a fork.

OKRA GRIDDLE CAKES

Fried okra was one of the southern staples I missed most when I was banned from good ol' fashioned batter fried foods. This recipe is a heartier version of my old favorite that works well even as a main dish.

2 cups thinly sliced okra
¼ cup dried chopped onion or ½ cup freshly chopped onion
½ cup cornmeal
½ cup Nearly Normal Gluten-Free Flour Mix™
1 ½ tsp. salt
1 tsp. baking powder
1 egg, beaten
½ cup water
½ tsp. pepper
½ cup extra virgin olive oil

You will need 3 mixing bowls, one larger than the others, and a large skillet.

Mix the cornmeal, Nearly Normal Gluten-Free Flour Mix™, 1 tsp. salt and baking powder together in a large mixing bowl. In a smaller bowl, whisk together the egg and water. Stir the egg mixture into the larger bowl, mixing with the dry ingredients until the large lumps are smooth. Place the okra and chopped onion in another small bowl and sprinkle with the remaining salt and the pepper. Fold these vegetables into the large bowl batter.

Heat the oil in the skillet until hot, but not popping yet. Spoon the batter into the oil by heaping tablespoons and flatten slightly with the back side of the spoon. Fry each griddle cake until light brown on each side. Remove from the oil and drain on a platter lined with crumpled paper towels.*

*BAKING TIP: For any recipe calling for draining fried foods onto paper towels, make sure to use a high-quality paper towel, such as Viva, so that the towels don't rip apart and stick to your foods!

POLENTA FRENCH FRIES

My first exposure to polenta came as a child when my great-grandmother would make it from scratch and fry it up with syrup for breakfast. Despite being dubbed "mush" in West Virginia, it still tasted yummy! If you shop in West Virginia today, you can still buy mush in the grocery store for about ⅓ of what you'll pay in grocery stores elsewhere for "polenta." You must admit though, that "Mush Fries" just doesn't have the same ring to it! Whatever the name, this stuff is great fried, broiled or sautéed.

2 refrigerated tubes of plain polenta (or mush!)
3 Tbs. olive oil
Sea salt and coarsely ground pepper, to taste
1 tsp. dried oregano

Preheat oven to 450 F.

Prepare a baking sheet by spreading the olive oil evenly across it.

Over the sink, unwrap and cut each tube of polenta in half — as soon as you cut the package open, water will pour out, so be careful! Cut each cross-wise half in half again, but this time lengthwise, creating 8 wedges.

Arrange the polenta wedges on the baking sheet, sprinkling salt and pepper over top. Toss the wedges gently in the oil to disburse. Arrange the wedges so that a single layer is formed on the baking sheet.

Bake for approximately 45 minutes, turning once in the middle, until the wedges are lightly browned and crispy. Remove from the baking sheet onto a paper towel-lined plate.* Pat dry, then place in a serving bowl. Add the oregano onto the wedges and toss gently before serving.

*BAKING TIP: For any recipe calling for draining fried foods onto paper towels, make sure to use a high-quality paper towel, such as Viva, so that the towels don't rip apart and stick to your foods!

RICE CON QUESO

This recipe may actually be served as a main dish, particularly if there are vegetarians in your midst! Brown or white rice works equally well here.

1 cup cooked rice
15 oz. cooked black beans (1 can, rinsed)
½ cup green chilies, chopped (1 small can)
¼ cup chopped onion
¼ tsp. cumin
½ tsp. coriander
½ tsp. salt
1 cup Ricotta cheese (light or whole milk)
⅓ cup milk (any kind)
2 cups shredded Monterrey Jack or Cheddar Jack cheese

Preheat oven to 350 F.

Cook the rice according to package directions to make at least 1 cup of cooked rice. Pour into a large mixing bowl. Rinse and add the black beans to the rice. Add the chopped chilies, onions and spices and mix together well. In a small bowl mix together the Ricotta cheese, milk and 1 ½ cups of shredded cheese. Add mixture to the large rice bowl and stir. Pour the entire mixture into a greased 8 x 8 baking pan and bake for 20 minutes. Sprinkle the remaining shredded cheese on top and bake and additional 10 minutes.

SWEET POTATO CASSEROLE I

Sweet potatoes are one of the most versatile, healthy and yummy staples in a gluten-free diet. Here, they add flavor to a light and fluffy casserole that can be enjoyed hot out of the oven or cold straight from the pan as leftovers! I've included two variations of a casserole or soufflé, as well as three variations for toppings, depending on what you have on hand and your own personal tastes. Also, feel free to use canned sweet potatoes in lieu of boiling and peeling, if time doesn't permit.

3 cups sweet potatoes, boiled, peeled and mashed (or canned, drained and mashed)
1 cup white sugar
½ cup butter or margarine
3 eggs, beaten
1 tsp. vanilla extract
1 tsp. ground nutmeg
2 tsp. cinnamon
½ tsp. ground cloves
1 tsp. ginger
1 cup sour cream
pinch of baking soda
pinch of salt
1 cup raisins (optional)

Preheat oven to 350 F.

With a wooden spoon or mixer, stir the mashed sweet potatoes, sugar, butter, eggs, vanilla extract, spices and sour cream. Add raisins, if you choose. Mix well, then add the salt and baking soda. Spread the mixture into a greased 1 ½ quart baking dish. Bake uncovered for 35 – 45 minutes, until the center is no longer jiggly. Remove from the oven and add your topping of choice, as listed on the following page.

... toppings next page

Nearly Normal Cooking™ for Gluten-Free Eating

Coconut Topping:

Mix the following ingredients and sprinkle on top of casserole:

4 Tbs. melted butter or margarine
1 cup brown sugar
2 Tbs. Nearly Normal Gluten-Free Flour Mix™
½ cup chopped pecans
½ cup coconut

Place the casserole back into the oven for approximately 10 more minutes, until lightly browned.

Marshmallow Topping:

Sprinkle enough miniature marshmallows to cover the top of the casserole. Add a sprinkling of chopped pecans, if desired. Put the casserole back into the oven until the marshmallows melt and are lightly browned.

Pecan Topping:

The simplest of the three, yet perhaps the best! Just sprinkle chopped and whole pecans over the top of the casserole and add approximately 5 minutes more to the baking time.

SWEET POTATO CASSEROLE II

3 cups cooked or canned mashed sweet potatoes
1 tsp. vanilla extract
2 eggs – slightly beaten
1 cup white sugar
½ cup melted butter
1 tsp. cinnamon
½ tsp. nutmeg

Topping:
1 cup brown sugar (I prefer the dark brown sugar – more flavor).
½ cup chopped pecans
1/3 cup cornstarch or arrowroot
¼ cup melted butter

Preheat oven to 325 F.

Put all ingredients into a large mixing bowl and beat on medium speed until smooth. Pour into a greased 9 x 13 casserole dish and set aside. Prepare topping by combining all ingredients and mixing by hand. Sprinkle over top of the casserole and bake for 50 minutes.

SWEET POTATO SOUFFLÉ

3 cups sweet potatoes, boiled, peeled and mashed (or canned, drained and mashed)
¾ cup brown sugar
¼ cup white sugar
1 egg, slightly beaten
½ cup milk
2 Tbs. melted butter or substitute
1 tsp. vanilla extract
½ tsp. almond or butternut flavoring
1 tsp. cinnamon
¾ cup coconut

Topping:
4 Tbs. melted butter
¾ cup brown sugar
4 Tbs. Nearly Normal Gluten-Free Flour Mix™
½ cup chopped pecans
½ cup coconut

Preheat oven to 350 F.

Mix all ingredients well and place in an oblong baking dish that has been lightly buttered or oiled. Spread topping evenly over the soufflé and bake for 45 minutes.

Main Events

BAKED MARINATED CHICKEN WITH PEPPERS

This recipe makes a colorful and tasty chicken dinner that can be served with rice or gluten-free pasta.

1 chicken, about 3 to 3½ pounds (or just use pieces that you like)
2 lemons
about 10 sprigs of Italian parsley, leaves only
1 cup olive oil
Salt and freshly ground black pepper
3 green, orange, yellow or sweet red peppers

If using a whole chicken, cut it into 8 pieces and place them in a bowl. Squeeze the lemons and add the juice to the bowl with the chicken. Coarsely chop the parsley and add it to the bowl along with ½ cup of the oil. Sprinkle with salt and pepper. Mix together all the ingredients in the bowl with a wooden spoon and then let the chicken marinate for 1 hour, turning the pieces over after ½ hour.

Clean the peppers, removing the stems, ribs and seeds from the inside. Cut the peppers into rings less than ½ inch thick.

Preheat the oven to 400 F.

Use tongs to transfer the chicken pieces with some of the chopped parsley clinging to them from the bowl to a baking dish. Pour the remaining ¼ cup of oil over the chicken. Place the dish in the oven and bake for 35 minutes.

Meanwhile, transfer the marinade to a saucepan and heat it over medium heat. When the marinade is hot, add the peppers and sauté for about 20 minutes or until they are cooked but still firm. Add salt and pepper, to taste.

Remove the baking dish from the oven and transfer the chicken pieces to a serving dish. Arrange the peppers and sauce in a ring around the chicken. Serve immediately.

*BAKING TIP: You may refrigerate the chicken in the marinade for as long as you like — just be sure to take it out of the refrigerator about an hour before cooking and stir a few times during that hour.

BARBEQUED CHICKEN PIZZA

This recipe is great for a get together with friends to make your own pizzas. Have your gluten-free crust ready and use the regular crusts for the non-celiac guests (or they may even want yours instead!).

2 cups shredded cooked chicken breast
1 cup gluten-free barbeque sauce
12 in. purchased gluten-free pizza crust
      or one pre-baked recipe for gluten-free Pizza Crust (p. 67)
3 plum tomatoes, sliced
1 cup shredded Monterey Jack cheese (or more, if you're a cheese lover)
Fresh cilantro leaves (optional)

Preheat oven to 450 F.

Combine chicken and barbeque sauce; mix well. Place pizza crust on ungreased cookie sheet or a baking stone. Spread chicken mixture over shell. Arrange tomatoes over top and sprinkle with cheese.

Bake for 10 minutes or until cheese is melted.

CHICKEN REUBEN

4 chicken breasts
1 can sauerkraut, drained
1 can mushrooms, drained or 6 – 8 medium fresh, sliced mushrooms
Sliced Swiss cheese (4 – 6 slices)
Gluten-free Thousand Island dressing

Preheat oven to 300 F.

Place chicken in greased baking dish. Layer remaining ingredients over the chicken in the order listed. Cover and bake for approximately 1 ½ hours, or less if the chicken is boneless.

CRAB & ASPARAGUS MINI CASSEROLES

This is a fun recipe to take to a dinner gathering, since each couple can share a mini casserole as part of the meal! I have offered some suggested alternative ingredients, but this recipe is one in which other substituted veggies would work well too.

10 – oz. package of frozen asparagus, 2 cans cut and drained asparagus
      or 1 bunch fresh, steamed asparagus
1 cup fresh, sliced mushrooms, 2 small cans of portabella mushrooms
      or 1 small jar of drained artichoke hearts

¼ cup onion, finely chopped	1 Tbs. margarine or butter
1 Tbs. cornstarch	dash of salt
dash of nutmeg	dash of black pepper
1 cup milk (skim is fine)	½ cup shredded Mozzarella cheese
8 oz. crabmeat, cleaned and drained	2 Tbs. toasted almonds, chopped
2 Tbs. fresh grated Parmesan or Asiago cheese	

Preheat oven to 400 F.

If using frozen asparagus, cook per package directions; for canned asparagus, drain; for fresh asparagus, steam and drain. Cut the asparagus spears into bite-sized chunks and set aside.

In a medium-sized frying pan, sauté the onions in margarine or butter until the onion is tender, but not yet browned. If using fresh mushrooms, cook them with the onion in margarine. If using canned mushrooms or artichoke hearts, drain, then stir them in after cooking the onion. Next add the cornstarch, salt, pepper and nutmeg. After mixing well, stir in the milk over medium-low heat until thickened and bubbly. Cook while stirring for one minute more, then add the Mozzarella cheese, crab and asparagus.

Spoon all into four small oiled casserole dishes; this is important, as the mixture becomes too watery if it is all combined into a large casserole. Sprinkle the tops with an equal mixture of toasted almonds and cheese. Bake for 10 minutes, or until the cheese is browned on the tops. Serve warm.

CRAB CRÊPES

Living as I do in Baltimore, it is always a challenge to find new ways to use crab in my cooking. Blue crab here is as lobster is to Maine and as crawfish is to Louisiana. One school of thought is that everything tastes better if you add crabmeat -- this recipe certainly does!

<u>Crêpes:</u>
2 Tbs. Nearly Normal Gluten-Free Flour Mix™
3 eggs, slightly beaten
3 Tbs. milk
½ tsp. salt

Prepare a small frying pan by heating it to medium-low heat and then adding one tablespoon of butter or margarine.

Combine all the crêpe ingredients in a small bowl, mixing until there are no lumps.

When the butter has melted, pour a thin layer of batter onto the pan. Pick up the pan and move it around until all the batter spreads out thinly and begins to set. Cook for only about one minute, or until the batter is completely set on the bottom. Flip the crêpe over gently and cook for only a half of a minute on the other side. Do not burn! Set crêpe aside, cover and repeat until all batter is used. (Makes approximately 6 – 8 6-inch crêpes).

<u>Crab mixture:</u>
½ lb. cleaned crabmeat
      (or you may use peeled shrimp or other seafood of your choice)
2 Tbs. butter or margarine
1 Tbs. lemon juice
¼ tsp. sea salt
¼ tsp. black pepper
½ tsp. fresh parsley
grated Parmesan, to taste

Using a small saucepan, melt the butter then add the crabmeat. Cook until heated, coating the crabmeat with butter. Add the remaining ingredients, stirring thoroughly. Remove from the heat and spoon dollops of the crab mixture into each crêpe. Fold two sides of the crêpe over the filling and place two or three on each person's plate. Sprinkle the Parmesan over the top of the crêpes and drizzle any remaining warm lemon-butter from the pan on top. Serve immediately.

CRAB OR SHRIMP QUICHE WITH VEGETABLES

Not only is this quiche delicious, but it's easy to make because you don't have to worry about a crust! It's also a very forgiving recipe, so feel free to be creative. I've included several options for ingredients, but you may find others on hand that work just as well. This is a great, hearty meal for a chilly fall day!

½ cup sliced mushrooms (may use canned portabellas), zucchini, broccoli,
     corn, chopped red potatoes or other additions of your choosing
1 – 2 Tbs. butter or margarine
     (depending on the amount of additions you sauté)
4 eggs, lightly beaten
1 cup sour cream
     (light or fat free works just as well as whole milk sour cream)
1 cup Ricotta cheese or small curd cottage cheese
2 cups Mozzarella, Parmesan and Romano mixed, Monterey Jack
     or other mild shredded cheese
8 – 12 oz. shrimp (chopped, if large) or crabmeat
¼ cup rice flour
pinch of salt
1 tsp. parsley
1 tsp. oregano or basil (depending on your choice of cheese)

Preheat oven to 350 F.

Sauté butter and vegetables, legumes or mushrooms, or any combination thereof that you choose. Mix eggs, sour cream, Ricotta or cottage cheese, rice flour, salt and spices. Stir in your sautéed ingredients, shredded cheese and seafood. Pour mixture into a large greased quiche dish or deep pie plate. Depending on how many additions you used, you may need a small casserole prepared to handle the additional batter.

Bake for approximately 45 minutes, or until the center is no longer jiggly and a knife inserted into the center comes out clean.

CRABMEAT & ARTICHOKE CASSEROLE

I've experimented with this recipe since college, and it seems to be just as great in this gluten-free version.

¼ cup butter or margarine
2 Tbs. minced onion
¼ cup Nearly Normal Gluten-Free Flour Mix™
1 pint half and half
     (or 4 Tbs. melted butter + enough whole milk to total 1 pint)
⅓ cup sherry
1 Tbs. lemon juice
2 cups crabmeat
1 ½ packages artichoke hearts
1 ¼ cups gluten-free macaroni shells
     (cook according to package directions before adding)
1 cup grated Swiss or other cheese, to taste
1 Tbs. paprika
1 Tbs. pepper
2 tsp. salt

Preheat oven to 350 F.

Melt butter and sauté onions until light brown. Stir in Nearly Normal Gluten-Free Flour Mix™ and cook for two minutes. Remove from heat and add the half and half. Return to moderate heat and stir until the mixture boils and thickens. Reduce to low heat and add sherry and spices. Remove from heat and set aside.

Pour lemon juice over the crabmeat and combine with the cooked noodles and artichoke hearts. Stir sauce into mixture and pour all into greased casserole dish. Sprinkle the top with cheese and bake for 30 minutes.

CREOLE CRABMEAT CASSEROLE

I am always searching for meals I can prepare and serve for days to come. This casserole is like many that gets better after sitting for even one day. Feel free to add more seasoning, but the recipe provides a nice flavor as it is.

8 oz. crabmeat
1 cup instant, uncooked rice
1 onion, chopped
½ green, orange, yellow or red pepper, to taste
10 ½ oz. can of gluten-free tomato-based soup
2 Tbs. oil
2 Tbs. Worcestershire sauce
1 tsp. Tabasco or other hot sauce, to taste
1 tsp. salt
8 oz. can of tomatoes, chopped (roasted is best)
½ cup shredded Mozzarella cheese (optional)

Preheat oven to 325 F.

Combine all the ingredients (except Mozzarella) and place in a greased casserole dish. Cover with foil and bake for 35 minutes. Add shredded Mozzarella cheese and cook, uncovered for an additional five minutes.

DIJON CHICKEN

This recipe is quick, easy and doesn't require many ingredients – what more could you ask for dinner?

3 Tbs. butter or margarine
6 skinned, boned chicken breasts
14 ½ oz. can chicken broth
1 medium-sized sweet onion (like Vidalia), diced
3 Tbs. Nearly Normal Gluten-Free Flour Mix™
3 Tbs. dijon mustard

Melt butter in a large skillet over medium-high heat; add chicken and cook 2 minutes on each side or until golden brown. Whisk together remaining ingredients and pour over chicken in the skillet. Cover, reduce heat to low and simmer 20 minutes. Serve warm.

FISH STEW

This Mexican-inspired stew is heartier than you might imagine. It is amazingly fast and easy to make, and the rice is optional if you're running short on time or on extra hands!

1 large can of diced, drained tomatoes
¾ cup frozen corn
½ tsp. cumin
¼ cup chopped fresh cilantro + extra leaves for garnish,
        or ⅛ cup chopped dried cilantro
1 lb. new potatoes, washed and sliced
2 large shallots or sweet onions (like Vidalias), peeled and thinly sliced
1 tsp. olive oil
1 tsp. sea salt
½ tsp. coarsely ground pepper
pinch of red pepper flakes (optional)
1 lb. skinless cod, grouper or red snapper fillet, cut into 1 ½ inch chunks
1 cup cooked brown or white rice (optional)

Mix together the tomatoes, corn, cumin and cilantro in a medium-sized bowl and set aside.

Combine the sliced potatoes, sliced shallots or onions and oil in a 2 quart microwave-safe dish. Stir to distribute the oil, then arrange in an even layer and sprinkle half of the salt and pepper over top. Cover and microwave on high for 5-6 minutes, depending on how thinly the potatoes are sliced.

Arrange the fish chunks in a single layer around the outside of the dish, but still on top of the potatoes. Season with the remaining salt and pepper (add the red pepper here if you want extra spice). Pour the vegetable mixture into the middle of the dish. Cover again and microwave on high until the fish and potatoes are cooked through, approximately 9-10 minutes. Stir to combine everything. If using rice, add in the cooked rice or pour over a serving of cooked rice; otherwise, spoon into bowls and garnish with fresh cilantro leaves.

GALETTES

These pancakes originated in France and have always been made gluten-free! They are made with buckwheat flour and are good served plain or with a filling. Some galette recipes direct that the pancake be wrapped around a sausage (Galette Sausice), while others call for fillings such as cooked ham, cheese, tomatoes, smoked salmon, onion, crème fraiche, etc. Use your imagination and enjoy this traditional French treat! The only trick to this recipe is that the batter should be made in advance and allowed to sit for two hours.

1 cup buckwheat flour
pinch of salt
2 eggs, slightly beaten
2 cups cold water
3 Tbs. melted butter

Mix all of the ingredients in a medium- sized bowl and stir until it is smooth.

Let the batter rest for 2 hours.

Grease a large flat frying pan with butter or oil. Gently pour some of your batter into the heated pan and rotate it so that a very thin pancake forms. Flip once. When it is just cooked through, add your cooked fillings and flip the corners of the gallette over to form a square.

Slide out on to plate and serve on its own or with a green salad.

Nearly Normal Cooking™ for Gluten-Free Eating

GREEK CHICKEN

Because of the many ingredients in this recipe, it is easy to add or subtract to suit your own tastes. This is a very forgiving recipe!

12 oz. package of pitted, bite-size dried plums
3.5 oz. jar capers
1 Tbs. dried oregano
6 bay leaves
1 whole garlic bulb (not clove), minced (about 1 Tbs.)
½ cup pimento-stuffed olives or Kalamata olives
½ cup red wine vinegar
½ cup olive oil
1 Tbs. coarse sea salt
2 tsp. pepper
8 lbs. boneless chicken breasts
⅔ cup brown sugar
1 cup dry white wine
¼ cup fresh parsley, chopped (optional)

Combine the first 10 ingredients in a large zip-top freezer bag or a large bowl. Add chicken breasts, turning to coat well. Seal or cover and chill for at least 8 hours (overnight is best), turning chicken occasionally.

Preheat oven to 350 F.

After chilling, arrange chicken in a single layer in one or two large oblong baking dishes. Pour marinade evenly over the chicken and sprinkle evenly with brown sugar. Lastly, pour the wine around the chicken. Bake for 50 minutes to 1 hour, basting as needed to keep the chicken moist.

Remove chicken, dried plums, olives and capers to a serving platter. Drizzle with ¾ cup of the juices left from the baking pan. Sprinkle parsley evenly over top, if desired. Serve over rice mixed with remaining pan juices.

GRIDDLE CORN CAKES

These corn cakes can be an entrée themselves, served with your favorite salsa or guacamole, a side dish in place of rice or an appetizer for any Mexican meal. Their versatility makes it easy to use this recipe on a regular basis. Try adding black beans to the recipe for variation.

¾ cup cornmeal
½ cup Nearly Normal Gluten-Free Flour Mix™
2 Tbs. sugar
pinch of salt
1 tsp. baking powder
1 large beaten egg
2 Tbs. oil
1 cup buttermilk, milk or milk substitute
1 can corn kernels, drained
1 small handful chopped scallions or onions
½ tsp. ground black pepper
Salsa, taco sauce, guacamole or other topping

Combine the beaten egg, oil and buttermilk. Whisk together then fold in all dry ingredients to form a batter. Add most of the can of corn, the scallions or onion, and the pepper.

Preheat a lightly greased griddle or skillet over medium-high heat. Spoon the batter onto the hot surface in ½ cup measures. Cook each cake until the edges are lightly browned. Flip each browned pancake to the other side and continue cooking until the other side is also lightly browned. Remove to a warmed plate or cookie sheet and place in a warm oven until all cakes are done. Serve with your favorite topping.

HAWAIIAN CROCK-POT CHICKEN & RICE

A good friend of mine (who protests that she does not know how to cook) makes this dish frequently and swears that even she cannot mess it up... sounds like a great meal idea to me!

3 – 4 lb. whole roasting chicken
1 can chicken or vegetable broth
¼ tsp. garlic powder
1 tsp. sea salt
2 tsp. gluten-free soy sauce
1 large can of fruit cocktail
10 oz. jar of gluten-free sweet and sour sauce
2 Tbs. cold water
2 Tbs. cornstarch

(Steamed rice)

Wash the chicken and pat it dry. Sprinkle the salt and garlic powder into the cavity. Place the chicken in the crock-pot, brush it with soy sauce, pour the broth into the pot and then cover with the lid. Cook on low for 8-10 hours or on high for 4 – 5 hours.

One hour before serving, remove all but approximately ½ cup of broth with a baster. Ensure there is still enough broth to cover the bottom of the pot. In a small bowl, mix the water with the cornstarch to form a paste. Pour the canned fruit and sweet and sour sauce over the chicken, then add the paste in with the fruit and sauce. Cook on high for one hour more, or until the broth is thickened. Serve over steamed rice.

"HEALTHY" TACOS

1 Tbs. oil
1 small onion, chopped
4 ounces fresh sliced mushrooms
1 cup water
1 cup Textured Vegetable Protein ("TVP"), minced
2 Tbs. gluten-free commercial taco seasoning*
2 tomatoes, diced
1 small head romaine lettuce, cut into ribbons
1 cup sour cream or low fat yogurt
1 cup taco sauce
Six 6-inch soft corn tortillas or hard shell corn tacos

In a medium saucepan, heat the oil over medium heat. Add the onion and mushrooms and cook until the onion is translucent, stirring. Add the water, TVP and taco seasoning and bring to a simmer. Cook while stirring for about 10 minutes. Transfer the mixture to a warm serving bowl.

Dice and arrange the tomatoes, lettuce, sour cream/yogurt and taco sauce in individual serving bowls. Warm the corn tortillas in a lightly oiled skillet by sautéing on each side, or heat shells in a preheated oven on 375 F for about 7 minutes. Spoon servings of all ingredients into each tortilla or shell and serve immediately.

*If you cannot find any commercially available gluten-free taco seasoning, try this easy mixture:

1 tsp. chili powder
½ tsp. black pepper
½ tsp. cumin

½ tsp. salt
½ tsp. garlic powder

HERB RUBBED CHICKEN BREASTS

One of my more industrious chef friends has developed these delicious recipes for her catering business, and her customers sing their praises. I'm not allowed to tell them how easy these rubs are, but I've been given permission to pass the secrets on to you!

Each "Rub Recipe" is enough for 4 chicken breasts. They can be cooked in a skillet or on the grill. For sautéing instructions, see page 64. The chicken should be "rubbed" at least 2 hours in advance, longer if possible. Also, the breasts can be "rubbed" with the spices and then frozen, so all you have to do for dinner is thaw and cook.

To make scallopini, cut the chicken breasts in half horizontally - they end with two skinny pieces of meat that cook really fast. Also, because there is less meat in each bite, the flavors of the rub are more pronounced.

LEMON OREGANO CHICKEN BREASTS

<u>In small bowl mix:</u>
2 cloves garlic, pressed
1 Tbs. lemon pepper
1 Tbs. olive oil
1 ½ tsp. oregano, dried

Wearing gloves, rub mixture onto both sides of chicken breasts.

CHICKEN SCALOPPINI WITH FRESH GARDEN HERBS

<u>In small bowl mix:</u>
2 Tbs. tarragon, fresh, chopped
1 Tbs. parsley, fresh, chopped
2 cloves garlic, pressed
½ tsp. lemon pepper
½ tsp. salt
2 Tbs. olive oil

Wearing gloves, rub mixture onto both sides of chicken breasts.

TUSCAN HOT OIL CHICKEN

<u>In a small bowl mix:</u>
¼ cup olive oil
⅛ cup parsley, dried
1 tsp. pepper, red crushed
1 tsp. salt
2 cloves garlic, pressed

Wearing gloves, rub all over chicken breasts keeping chicken inside ziptop bag.

HONEY GARLIC WINGS

Craving some great wings? These finger-licking wings will have them begging for more!

½ cup honey
¼ tsp. lite gluten-free soy sauce
2 Tbs. ketchup
2 Tbs. canola oil
1 clove garlic, crushed (or more if you LOVE garlic)
2 lbs. chicken wings, thawed
Pepper to taste

Preheat oven to 350 F.

Place chicken in a foil-lined baking dish. Season with pepper. Combine ingredients well and pour over chicken. Bake for 1 hour.

*BAKING TIP: If you add 1 Tbs. of cornstarch 10 minutes before the end of the cooking period, it thickens the sauce and enhances the yummy, sticky, finger-licking good taste of these wings!

LEMON CHICKEN

This light chicken dish may be broiled, sautéed or microwaved. Marinate in a covered glass dish for as long as possible before cooking for maximum flavor.

6 boneless, skinless chicken breast halves
2 Tbs. lemon juice
2 Tbs. white wine
2 Tbs. olive oil
1 clove garlic, minced
1 tsp. honey
1 tsp. dried oregano
½ tsp. pepper
½ tsp. sea salt
Sliced lemon for garnish

Combine lemon juice, wine, 1 tablespoon olive oil, garlic, honey, oregano, salt and pepper. Pour into a shallow glass baking dish and add the chicken, turning to coat both sides. Cover and refrigerate for at least 30 minutes.

Sauté:
Heat remaining oil in a large skillet over medium heat. Add the chicken, discarding any excess marinade. Cook on both sides until it is no longer pink in the middle, approximately 20 minutes total.

Microwave:
Microwave on high, turning once, until chicken is no longer pink, or about 8 minutes.

Broil:
Place chicken on broiler, using remaining olive oil. Turn once, broiling on high until no longer pink in the middle. Broiler times will vary with your oven and the thickness of the chicken breasts, but be careful not to burn them!

MEXICAN LASAGNA

1 pound lean ground beef, ground turkey or firm tofu
½ cup chopped onion
½ cup chopped green, orange or sweet red peppers
2 ½ cups chunky salsa
8 ¾ oz. can of whole kernel corn, drained
1 tsp. chili powder
1 tsp. ground cumin
10 corn tortillas, cut in half
2 cups (16 oz.) small curd cottage cheese
1 cup sharp shredded Cheddar cheese
2 small cans of sliced, pitted ripe olives, drained (optional)

Preheat oven to 350 F.

Brown meat or tofu, onion and peppers in a large skillet on medium heat, then drain.
Add salsa, corn and seasonings. Layer 1/3 of the meat sauce, ½ of the tortillas and
½ of the cottage cheese in a 13 x 9 baking dish. Repeat the layers, ending with meat
sauce. Sprinkle with Cheddar cheese and olives. Bake for 30 minutes.

PECAN ENCRUSTED BAKED FISH

This fish recipe has got to be one of my all-time favorites. It works well with mahi mahi, snapper, grouper or other similar white fish. It is fun to serve with fresh tomatoes, mango salsa or other fresh salsa blend.

4 fish fillets
1 egg, beaten
½ cup milk
½ cup ground pecans
1 cup Nearly Normal Gluten-Free Flour Mix™
¼ cup grated Parmesan cheese (optional)

½ Tbs. cayenne pepper
½ Tbs. oregano
1 Tbs. paprika
1 Tbs. salt
½ Tbs. onion powder
½ Tbs. pepper

½ cup extra virgin olive oil

Preheat oven to 375 F.

You will need 1 small bowl, 3 bowls large enough for a fillet to fit into, 1 large ovenproof skillet and 1 ovenproof dish large enough to hold all the fillets.

Mix the spices together in a small bowl. Wash fish fillets and sprinkle a small amount of spices onto each fillet.

In the first of the three other bowls, mix ½ cup Nearly Normal Gluten-Free Flour Mix™ and 1 Tbs. spice mixture. In the second bowl, add together the beaten egg and milk. In the third bowl, combine the ground pecans, ½ cup Nearly Normal Gluten-Free Flour Mix™, Parmesan cheese and 1 Tbs. spice mixture.

Heat the olive oil in the oven-proof skillet over high heat on your stove top.

Meanwhile, dredge each seasoned fillet in the first bowl, then in the second egg wash bowl then lastly in the third pecan-flour bowl.

Place each fillet into the oil when it is hot. Sauté until golden brown on each side — approximately 1-2 minutes each. Place each fillet into the ovenproof dish and cook in the oven until the fish is crisp — approximately 5 minutes. Serve with fresh tomatoes or salsa.

PIZZA
(makes 1 crust)

1 ½ cups of Nearly Normal Gluten-Free Flour Mix™
3 Tbs. milk powder
¼ tsp. oregano
Pinch or two of garlic powder
½ tsp. salt
2 ½ tsp. yeast
2 egg whites
2 Tbs. olive oil
½ tsp. cider vinegar
¾ cup warm water, more or less

Blend dry ingredients. Combine wet ingredients and blend, reserving some of the water. Turn the mixer to low and add the Nearly Normal Gluten-Free Flour Mix™. Add more water as needed to get a firm dough that can still be spread. Beat on high for 3 minutes.

Preheat oven to 400 F.

Spoon the dough onto a greased pizza pan or baking stone reserved for gluten-free cooking only (I like the results of the baking stone). Spread into a 12 inch circle using a flat spoon. Raise the edges so the topping won't fall off. Let rise about 10 minutes and then bake for about 15 minutes. Cooking time will vary depending on your pan. Spread with pizza sauce, toppings and cook an additional 20 minutes, or until the cheese is bubbly. If you add vegetable toppings, I find they taste best if you sauté them in olive oil before adding to the crust.

POTATO ENCRUSTED FISH

This recipe works well with any mild white fish like cod or halibut, and its presentation masks its deceptive simplicity!

12 ounces thick fish filet
1 small white potato (+/- 5 ounces)
Sea salt and black pepper to taste
¼ tsp. crushed dried rosemary leaves
1 Tbs. extra virgin olive oil

Rinse the fish under cold running water and pat dry. Sprinkle with salt and pepper to taste. Peel the potato and grate over the large holes of a cheese grater. Make sure any excess water is squeezed out of the potato at this point. Season the potato with salt, pepper and rosemary; press it around the fish.

In a non-stick pan, heat olive oil over medium heat. Gently slide the fish into the pan. If any potato falls off, cook next to the fish and serve with the fish on the plate. Cook for 3 to 5 minutes, turn and cook for 3 to 5 minutes more or until potatoes are golden and the fish is flaky in the middle. This recipe is nice served with steamed asparagus or another fresh green vegetable.

QUESADILLAS

This dish is my favorite. As a non-meat eater with little extra time on my hands, I seem to make some kind of a quesadilla for lunch nearly every time I'm home or have anyone over. It is so easy to add different ingredients to change the flavor, and it makes a low-fat alternative that even non-vegetarians seem to love. I have included two of my favorite variations, but feel free to experiment and devise your own concoctions - Mexican food is very forgiving! Just be sure to include some salsa and cheese, and voila!

BLACK BEAN QUESADILLAS

1 can black beans, rinsed and drained
½ cup chunky salsa
¼ cup sweet corn kernels
½ pound Pepper-Jack, Mozzarella, Cheddar or a mixture of cheeses, shredded
1 package Sazón Goya seasoning or gluten-free taco seasoning*
¼ cup guacamole (optional)
8 8-inch corn tortillas
Parmesan cheese

In a pot over medium heat, add all ingredients except for the cheese and guacamole. Stir to mix and cover until mixture is cooked through, but not boiling. Remove from heat and set aside.

Place tortillas individually in a small skillet oiled or sprayed with gluten-free cooking spray. Cook over low heat on each side until the tortillas are slightly browned, but not crunchy. Lay one cooked tortilla back onto the oiled skillet and spoon ¼ of the bean mixture and the cheese. Place another cooked tortilla on top of this mixture and sprinkle with Parmesan. Turn quesadilla over using a large spatula, sprinkle with Parmesan, and cook on the other side until the cheese begins to melt. Serve on individual plates garnished with guacamole and salsa. Add rice as a side dish, if desired, and cook per directions above.

*If you cannot find any commercially available gluten-free taco seasoning, try this easy mixture:

1 tsp. chili powder
½ tsp. black pepper
½ tsp. cumin

½ tsp. salt
½ tsp. garlic powder

RICE AND MUSHROOM QUESADILLAS

2 cups brown rice, cooked per package directions
4 cups water
oil
½ pound fresh mushrooms (whichever type you prefer — different mushrooms
        provide totally different flavor)
1 small yellow onion or ½ cup dried onion flakes
2 tsp. garlic powder
8 8-inch corn tortillas
½ pound Pepper-Jack cheese, thinly sliced
1 cup crumbled feta cheese (optional)
¼ cup salsa
¼ cup guacamole (optional)
Parmesan cheese

Heat 2 Tbs. oil in large skillet over high heat. Trim and slice the mushrooms while the oil is heating. Add the mushrooms and onions and sprinkle in the garlic. Sauté for 5 minutes, or until the onion is translucent. Set aside to cool.

Place tortillas individually in a small skillet oiled or sprayed with non-stick cooking spray. Cook over low heat on each side until the tortillas are slightly browned, but not crunchy. Lay one cooked tortilla back onto the oiled skillet and spoon ¼ of each of the rice, mushroom mixture, Pepper-Jack cheese, feta cheese and salsa. Place another cooked tortilla on top of this mixture and sprinkle Parmesan cheese. Turn quesadilla over using a large spatula, sprinkle with Parmesan, and cook on the other side until the cheese begins to melt. Serve on individual plates garnished with guacamole and salsa.

ROASTED VEGETABLE LASAGNA

This is another one of those very forgiving recipes that comes in handy when you need to clean out your refrigerator! I list ingredients here that have worked well for me, but feel free to substitute whatever vegetables you have on hand.

1 box gluten-free lasagna noodles, cooked according to package directions
2 Tbs. olive oil
1 Tbs. dried oregano
1 tsp. crushed garlic
1 tsp. sea salt
½ cup diced fresh onions or ¼ cup diced dried onions
2 – 3 cups fresh zucchini slices, cut in half
2 red, orange, yellow and/or green peppers, chopped
1 cup diced mushrooms
1 large tomato, chopped
⅓ cup milk
8 oz. shredded and/or sliced Mozzarella cheese
1 ½ cups Ricotta or cottage cheese
1 jar chunky commercial pasta sauce
½ cup grated Parmesan cheese

Preheat oven to broil.

Cook pasta, rinse and set aside.

Chop all vegetables except tomatoes and arrange on a greased baking sheet. Sprinkle with garlic, spices and oil. Place in the oven and broil, stirring occasionally, until the zucchini is tender and lightly browned. Add the tomatoes for 2 minutes more.

Remove pan and reduce oven temperature to 350 F.

In a small bowl, mix the Ricotta or cottage cheese and milk together and set aside.

In an ungreased baking pan (13 x 9) pour ⅓ of the pasta sauce to cover the bottom of the pan. Squeeze any excess liquid from the rinsed noodles and arrange 3 rows of noodles over the sauce. Add half of the roasted vegetables, then half of the Ricotta/cottage cheese mixture, then ⅓ of the Mozzarella and Parmesan cheeses. Repeat these layers once more, then add 3 more lasagna noodle rows and the remaining pasta sauce. Top with the remaining Mozzarella and Parmesan cheeses. Cover and bake for approximately 30 minutes.

SALMON & VEGETABLES
in Foil

4 – 6 to 8 oz. salmon fillets, preferably skinned
4 tsp. fresh lemon juice
2 tsp. minced fresh ginger (optional, but I wouldn't omit)
Salt and pepper to taste
2 Tbs. extra virgin olive oil
2 red or white potatoes, sliced and boiled
1 cup snow peas, blanched in boiling water for 30 seconds
2 carrots, thinly sliced, blanched in boiling water for 1 min.
¼ small zucchini, sliced
fresh, uncooked spinach leaves (optional)

(Note: Alternative vegetables include 1 cup peas, 1 cup corn, 8 stalks blanched asparagus, some sliced eggplant, etc.)

Optional: 4 tsp. Chopped <u>fresh</u> dill, basil, thyme or parsley for garnish

Preheat oven to 400 F.

Cut four sheets of aluminum foil. Splash a little olive oil on each sheet and place fillets on foil (or on top of spinach leaves on top of the foil), slightly off center. Sprinkle each fillet with 1 tsp. lemon juice, ½ tsp. ginger, salt and pepper. Top each fillet with ¼ of the vegetables, drizzle a little oil over them and add a little more salt and pepper, if desired. Fold foil over to form a rectangle and crimp all edges tightly. (If preparing ahead, stop here and refrigerate, then increase cooking time by 5 minutes.

Bake on cookie sheet(s) for 15 – 20 minutes or until fish is just cooked through. Serve with herb garnish.

SPICY SALMON

This recipe is a welcome alternative to the lemon pepper spices so commonly used on salmon.

6 – 8 pieces of salmon filets
1 Tbs. salt
1 Tbs. pepper
2 tsp. paprika
1 tsp. chile powder
2 tsp. sugar
3 Tbs. olive oil
½ tsp. garlic powder
½ tsp. onion powder

Thaw fillets in your refrigerator for 6 – 8 hours if possible, or for quicker thawing, place fillets in a zippered plastic bag (squeezing all the air out) and place under cold running water. Mix the seasonings together and rub liberally over the fish. Let sit for 1 – 3 hours.

Barbeque:
Remove excess rub mixture and grill for 3 – 4 minutes on each side.

Oven Broiled:
Place in a baking pan under the broiler for 6 – 8 minutes with the oven door cracked open.

Pan Fry:
Preheat a flat bottom non-stick pan to medium heat with 3 Tbs.vegetable oil. Place each fillet in oil and cook each side for 3 – 4 minutes or until done.

SPICY SHRIMP

2 garlic cloves, peeled and chopped
1 piece of fresh ginger, peeled and chopped
Fresh shrimp, peeled & de-veined
3 Tbs. vegetable oil
3 Tbs. tomato paste
½ tsp. ground turmeric
1 Tbs. lemon juice
¾ tsp. salt
¼ tsp. cayenne pepper

Put the garlic and ginger in a blender along with 3 tablespoons water. Blend at high speed until it becomes a smooth paste.

Wash shrimp well and pat dry. Cut each shrimp into 3 sections (optional). Set aside.

Heat oil in 10 – 12 inch skillet over medium heat. When hot, pour in the paste from the blender and fry, stirring constantly for 2 minutes. Add tomato paste and turmeric. Fry and stir another 2 minutes. Add 4 tablespoons water, the lemon juice, salt and cayenne pepper. Cover and simmer gently for 2 – 3 minutes.

(This much can be done in advance.)

Five minutes before serving, lift off cover, put in the shrimp and turn heat to high. Stir and fry the shrimp for about 5 minutes or until they just turn opaque.

Either place on a platter with a toothpick in each shrimp, or serve a portion on a bed of lettuce on a salad plate.

SPINACH CRUST PIZZA

There are very few things I miss as much as a fresh hot pizza delivered to my door. I will not tell you that a spinach crust pizza is a good substitute, but it is a fun way to get your cheese, tomato sauce and favorite toppings, as well as a low carb, high nutrient alternative. This recipe can also make a layer for your favorite casserole ingredients, or the crust for a quiche. For bread crumbs, I always keep the remnants of a loaf I bake, or an experiment gone bad, crush it into crumbs and freeze them for just such a recipe.

1 bag frozen or approximately 16 oz. fresh spinach leaves
2 eggs, beaten
1+/- cup finely ground gluten-free bread crumbs (to taste)
½ cup shredded Parmesan cheese
cornmeal

Preheat oven to 450 F.

Heat pizza stone in oven for ten minutes. Remove and dust with cornmeal, then prepare pizza on the stone.

Reduce temperature to 375 F.

Rinse and drain whole or chopped spinach leaves.
Mix with blended eggs, cheese and the bread crumbs. Add more or less bread crumbs according to how watery your spinach is and to your taste.
Spread the mixture across a pizza stone just as you would a pizza crust.

Bake for about 10 minutes, in 375 F oven, just until it starts to set.
Top with your favorite tomato sauce, cheese and other toppings and return to the oven until the cheese is bubbly.

*The crust works best when baked on a pizza stone, as the stone absorbs any excess moisture from the spinach. However, if you do not have a pizza stone, you may use a regular cookie sheet dusted with cornmeal.

SWEDISH VEGETABLE HASH

This recipe is a great one for dumping in all of the veggies that are getting ready to spoil in your refrigerator. I've listed suggested vegetable ingredients, but feel free to improvise and improve!

6 eggs, lightly beaten
1 Tbs. margarine or butter
¾ cup chopped red, orange, yellow or green peppers
¼ cup chopped green onions
2 Tbs. chopped fresh chives or 1 Tbs. dried chopped chives
1 Tbs. chopped fresh dill weed or 1 tsp. dried dill weed
¾ lb. new potatoes, cooked and cut into fourths (canned potatoes are fine)
½ can new peas
1 cup chopped tomatoes
1 cup fresh or 1 can chopped asparagus
½ cup plain yogurt (optional)
¾ cup shredded Mozzarella, Cheddar, Monterey Jack, Colby or other mild cheese

Melt the butter in a 10-inch skillet over medium heat. Cook the peppers, onions, chives and fresh asparagus for approximately 2 minutes. Stir in the eggs and dill. Cook until the eggs are thickened, but not overly dry. Stir in the potatoes, peas and canned asparagus and cook until heated. Serve warm onto individual plates, topping with chopped tomatoes, yogurt and cheese.

Nearly Normal Cooking™ for Gluten-Free Eating

TAMALE PIE

This easy recipe makes a beautiful pie that can be served as the entrée or as a colorful accompaniment to your meal. This recipe actually makes two pies and freezing one is a great solution to another night's meal dilemma!

2 ½ cups fine corn flour
2 cups milk or milk substitute
1 tsp. turmeric (you may substitute ½ tsp. dried mustard)
2 tsp. oil
1 medium onion, diced
1 ½ cups red, yellow, orange and green peppers, seeded and diced
15 oz. can crushed or diced tomatoes
15 oz. can black beans, rinsed and drained
1 Tbs. gluten-free taco seasoning*
1 cup shredded Cheddar cheese

Preheat oven to 400 F.

Combine the corn flour, milk and turmeric in a bowl, blending into a moist dough.

Spread ½ the dough in each of two lightly greased 9-inch pie pans. Spread evenly over the bottoms and up the sides of each pan. Cook these crusts for approximately 13 minutes, or until the crusts are dry. Remove from the oven and set aside.

In a large saucepan, heat the oil over medium heat and cook the onion and peppers until the onion is translucent. Stir in the tomatoes, beans and taco seasoning and simmer for 10 minutes, stirring occasionally.

Spoon the bean mixture over the tops of each crust, spreading evenly. Sprinkle each pie with cheese and return to the oven for 5 minutes, or until the cheese is bubbly. Remove from the oven and serve in pie pieces.

*If you cannot find any commercially available gluten-free taco seasoning, try this easy mixture:

1 tsp. chili powder   ½ tsp. salt
½ tsp. black pepper   ½ tsp. garlic powder
½ tsp. cumin

Quick & Yeast Breads

BANANA BLUEBERRY MUFFINS

I must have tried 20 different variations on banana bread recipes before I finally devised what are now my son's favorite muffins. I always seem to have over-ripe bananas in my kitchen, so we usually have these muffins at least once every other week. These are light, flavorful and not hard to make. This recipe calls for unflavored gelatin to help the batter hold together; for a vegetarian recipe, simply omit the packet of gelatin — the muffins will fall a bit when they come out of the oven, but they still taste good. The recipe makes approximately 16 muffins, depending on how full you like to fill your muffin cups, so be sure to have more than one pan available for cooking. If you choose to use muffin liners, it is helpful to lightly spray them with non-stick cooking spray before you fill them, otherwise, be sure to spray or otherwise grease the cups themselves.

1 ½ cups Nearly Normal Gluten-Free Flour Mix™
1 ½ tsp. baking soda   3 tsp. baking powder
pinch of salt   1 envelope unflavored gelatin*
2 tsp. cinnamon   ⅓ cup shortening
⅓ cup sugar   3 eggs, lightly beaten
1 tsp. vanilla extract   ¼ cup pecans (optional)
2 mashed bananas   1 cup fresh or frozen blueberries
1 tsp. grated lemon peel (optional)
¾ cup (6 oz.) yogurt (vanilla or other fruit flavor works best)

Preheat the oven to 350 F.

Sift together dry ingredients and set aside. Cream shortening, sugar, eggs and vanilla extract thoroughly, until the mixture is light. Add the mashed banana and yogurt, then slowly add the flour mixture, beating until mixed through. Add optional ingredients and blueberries last, by folding into the batter, so as not to damage the berries.

Pour into prepared muffin tins and bake for about 30 minutes, until the tops are lightly browned.

*BAKING TIP: For a completely vegetarian recipe, omit the gelatin.

      Nearly Normal Cooking™ for Gluten-Free Eating

BANANA BREAD

This recipe works particularly well when used in small loaf pans or even muffins. It produces a dense, moist and quite flavorful bread which does not fall much and is never crumbly. The addition of berries like cranberries or blueberries, while not necessary, provides extra flavor to suit the season.

½ cup butter or shortening
1 cup sugar
2 eggs
1 ½ cups Nearly Normal Gluten Free Flour Mix™
1 tsp. baking soda
2 tsp. baking powder
dash of salt
½ cup sour cream
1 tsp. vanilla
1 cup mashed, ripe banana
½ cup chopped pecans (optional)
½ cup berries (optional)

Preheat oven to 350 F.

Cream the butter or shortening and sugar until the mixture is light and fluffy. Add the eggs and beat well. Sift the dry ingredients together and add to the butter mixture. Blend well before adding the sour cream, vanilla and bananas. Add the nuts and berries, if using, just before pouring into greased loaf pans or muffin tins.

Bake for approximately 1 hour – less if using smaller pans. Test with a cake tester before removing from the oven to cool.

BREAD STICKS

The wonder of these bread sticks is not even how "normal" they taste when they come out of the oven, but how great they still taste the next day! Play with this recipe by shaping and topping the sticks with different seasoned salts, cheese, chopped nuts, seeds or other variations to accompany your meals. You can also shape the dough into pretzels and brush with an egg white mixture before baking, or use the same dough to make dinner rolls or even a loaf of bread! The yummy possibilities are endless!

¾ tsp. apple cider vinegar
¼ cup shortening
3 Tbs. honey
2 eggs
1 Tbs. yeast
1 cup vanilla yogurt
2 cups Nearly Normal Gluten-Free Flour Mix™
½ tsp. baking soda
2 tsp. baking powder
pinch of salt
topping of choice

Preheat oven to 350 F.

Combine all ingredients, mixing with a dough hook until the lumps are removed from the dough. Dust the counter or pastry mat with cornstarch, then dust your hands with cornstarch as well. Grab chunks of the wet dough, rolling it in cornstarch and your toppings into the shape you desire. Lay the sticks, pretzels or other shaped dough onto a greased baking sheet. Sprinkle with remaining toppings and bake for 10-12 minutes, or until the tops are lightly browned and the dough has risen.

BELGIAN WAFFLES

These light, airy waffles bake nicely in a traditional waffle iron. Be sure the iron is preheated and greased before pouring in the batter! Serve with fresh berries, Confectioner's sugar or syrup.

2 eggs, separated
2 Tbs. shortening
2 Tbs. oil
¼ cup sugar
1 ½ cups Nearly Normal Gluten-Free Flour Mix™
2 tsp. baking powder
½ tsp. salt
1 tsp. cinnamon
1 tsp. vanilla extract
¾ cup milk

Preheat and grease the waffle iron with non-stick cooking spray.

Have one medium bowl and one larger bowl ready for mixing. Into the medium bowl, pour the egg whites and beat until stiff peaks form, but the whites are not yet dry. Set aside.

In the larger bowl, combine the remaining ingredients in the order listed above. Mix while slowly adding the ingredients. Finally, fold in the stiff egg whites to the larger bowl.

Pour enough batter into the iron to cover the bottom — approximately ⅔ cup. Remove as soon as the waffle has separated from the iron and is a light brown color. Do not overcook!

Serve immediately and enjoy!

CARROT & ZUCCHINI BREAD

This bread is a colorful option to more traditional loaves. I often buy extra zucchini when it is fresh and in season, grate it and freeze the amount I need for each type of bread in individual baggies. That way, when I want some pretty breads to serve at the holidays, I can thaw a bag of zucchini and toss it in!

1 ½ cups Nearly Normal Gluten-Free Flour Mix™
¾ cup light brown sugar
1 Tbs. baking powder
½ tsp. baking soda
¼ tsp. salt
2 eggs, beaten slightly
¼ cup oil
¼ cup vanilla yogurt
½ cup grated carrots
1 ¾ cup grated zucchini
½ cup golden raisins

Preheat oven to 350 F.

Grease and "flour" a loaf pan with cornstarch . Combine eggs, yogurt and oil, mixing well. Sift the dry ingredients and combine with the egg mixture. Fold carrots, zucchini and raisins into the mixture. Pour into loaf pan and bake for 55 minutes or until a cake tester comes out clean. Remove to a wire rack and remove from pan after cooling for 5 minutes. Return to the rack to cool completely before slicing.

CRANBERRY BREAD 1

I am always searching for good quick bread recipes, and this is one of the best! I love the way it smells fresh out of the oven, and it tastes just as good! I like to make several small loaves of these and give them as gifts at the holidays.

1 egg
½ cup sugar
¼ cup oil
½ cup orange juice
½ cup milk or milk substitute (skim is ok to use too)
1 ⅔ cup Nearly Normal Gluten-Free Flour Mix™
1 ½ Tbs. baking powder
½ tsp. baking soda
⅔ cup+ chopped frozen cranberries
        (if the berries are not frozen, it just makes a mess!)
cinnamon-sugar for topping, to taste

Preheat oven to 350 F.

Mix the egg, sugar, oil, orange juice and milk, then all the dry ingredients, saving the cranberries for last. Mix all the ingredients well to remove any lumps, then gently stir in the cranberries. Pour batter into 1 large greased loaf pan or 4 small greased loaf pans. Sprinkle with cinnamon-sugar, to taste. Bake for 30-45 minutes, depending on the size of your pans. This bread is done when a skewer or cake tester inserted in the center of the loaf is clean when removed. The tops should be lightly browned. If your oven cooks too fast, you may want to cover the loaves with foil for the last 15 minutes to prevent overcooking the tops. Cool in the pans before removing.

CRANBERRY BREAD II

Cooking with cranberries, as with pumpkin, always signals the advent of cooler nights and shorter days. The tart flavor of fresh cranberries is a welcome treat in my baked goods, and I have sought as many recipes as I can find to add the berries for flavor. Although I prefer using fresh cranberries in baking, I recommend freezing them before you chop them to save on mess. This bread is a good one in the quick bread variety; feel free to add less or more berries to suit your own taste.

3 cups Nearly Normal Gluten-Free Flour Mix™
pinch of salt
2 tsp. powdered egg replacer (optional)
3 tsp. baking powder
1 tsp. baking soda
2 tsp. grated orange peel
1 cup sugar
1 ¼ cups yogurt
¾ cup orange juice
1 tsp. vanilla extract
½ tsp. orange oil (optional)
3 eggs and 1 egg white
4 Tbs. softened butter or margarine
2 Tbs. honey
1 tsp. apple cider vinegar
2 cups chopped cranberries
1 cup chopped walnuts or pecans (optional)

Preheat oven to 350 F.

Whisk together all dry ingredients and blend with the remaining ingredients. Add cranberries and nuts and spoon into four small greased bread pans.
Bake for 40 to 50 minutes.

Nearly Normal Cooking™ for Gluten-Free Eating

CRANBERRY BREAD WITH ORANGE

As an alternative to the more traditional cranberry breads, try this one with a heavy emphasis on orange flavor.

1 egg
¼ cup vanilla yogurt
½ cup orange juice (with pulp is best)
½ cup milk
½ cup sugar
1 ⅔ cup Nearly Normal Gluten-Free Flour Mix™
2 Tbs. baking powder
¼ tsp. baking soda
pinch of salt
⅔ cup finely chopped frozen cranberries
cinnamon-sugar for topping
grated orange peel (optional)
chopped nuts (optional)

Preheat oven to 350 F.

Mix the egg, sugar, yogurt, orange juice and milk. Add all other ingredients except the cranberries, mixing until all lumps are removed from the batter.

Fold in the cranberries, orange peel and nuts.

Pour into a large greased loaf pan or greased or lined muffin pans and sprinkle cinnamon-sugar over the batter before baking.

Bake for 40 minutes for bread, less for the muffins, depending on your oven. The bread is done when the tops are lightly browned and a cake tester or toothpick inserted into the center of the bread comes out clean. Cool in pans before removing.

HUSH PUPPIES

When I learned that I could no longer eat wheat, one of the first things I knew I would miss was the free basket of hot melt-in-your mouth hush puppies found on every table at seafood restaurants in eastern North Carolina. Calabash style hush puppies usually include wheat flour in the mix, but this one is just as tasty and satisfies any hush puppy cravings!

1 lb. corn meal
1 egg
1 Tbs. salt
1 Tbs.+ sugar
pinch of baking soda
1 cup buttermilk
oil for frying

Stir all ingredients, adding water until a thick consistency is achieved. Drop by teaspoonfuls into hot (375 F) oil and turn until entire hush puppy is fried to a golden brown. Allow to cool on paper towels to soak up any excess oil and enjoy with your favorite seafood meal.

Nearly Normal Cooking™ for Gluten-Free Eating

MONKEY BREAD

This is a great recipe to make when you have some extra fruit sitting around that needs to get eaten! Be creative with your additions and enjoy the variations of this sweet quick bread.

1 ½ cups Nearly Normal Gluten-Free Flour Mix™
1 cup sugar
1 tsp. baking soda
2 tsp. baking powder
1 tsp. cinnamon
1 tsp. vanilla
1 egg, slightly beaten
¼ cup melted shortening or butter
1 medium banana, mashed
1 ½ cups chopped, peeled fresh fruit (not citrus)*
1 cup chopped pecans

Preheat oven to 350 F.

Combine dry ingredients and slowly add the beaten egg and butter until moistened. Fold in the mashed banana, fresh fruit and pecans. Spoon the thick batter into greased loaf pans and bake for 45 minutes, or until a cake tester inserted into the center comes out clean. These breads will fall as they cool, so be prepared for a little visual let down!

*BAKING TIP: Good fruit options include one apple + two pears; one apple + two plums; one peach, one apple and one pear; one apple + one-half cup berries. If you use extremely juicy fruit, it should be drained before adding to the batter.

PANCAKES

One of my favorite things to do on a weekend morning has always been to make pancakes. I always add fresh fruit to mine, and I sometimes make them into shapes by using a cookie cutter after they have been fried. I have tried the pancake molds, but the mess doesn't seem to be worth the results! Like most pancake recipes, add more or less milk, depending on how thick you like your pancakes to be.

Preheat frying pan to medium heat and grease with shortening, butter or oil, to taste.

¾ cup Nearly Normal Gluten-Free Flour Mix™
1 Tbs. sugar
½ tsp. baking powder
pinch of salt
1 beaten egg
1 cup +/- milk
2 Tbs. oil
¼ cup fresh or frozen berries (optional)

Sift dry ingredients together and set aside. Mix liquids and add to dry mix. Stir just until blended, but still slightly lumpy.

In a large skillet, pour batter onto heated oil or butter, but do not let the pancake be too thick, or it will not cook all the way through. Fry each side just until the edges are lightly browned, then turn. Keep the cooked pancakes warm by placing directly onto a cookie sheet in a warm oven until all are ready to serve. Sprinkle with Confectioner's sugar or use maple syrup and enjoy!

BUCKWHEAT PANCAKES

Using the same recipe as above, use ¼ cup buckwheat flour and ½ cup Nearly Normal Gluten-Free Flour Mix™.

RICOTTA PANCAKES

Using the same recipe as above, add ½ cup Ricotta cheese, ½ cup water and an additional 1 Tablespoon of sugar. Do not add the oil or milk to the recipe.

PARMESAN PITAS

This recipe makes either a large thick pita round or several smaller, thinner rounds. I suggest making the smaller ones, as the size is more manageable and the breads become crispier around the edges. Cut each pita round as you would a pizza and use the wedges for dipping in your favorite sauce or appetizer dip. If you cut the wedges and still find that the middle is not crispy enough, lay out the wedges on a baking sheet and return to the oven for an additional 5 minutes, or until they are crispy but not burned.

1 cup milk
1 cup brown rice flour or ½ cup brown rice flour and ½ cup buckwheat flour
2 Tbs. melted butter

1 cup Nearly Normal Gluten-Free Flour Mix™
2 eggs
¾ cup yogurt
2 tsp. sea salt
1 yeast packet
2 tsp. grated Parmesan cheese

Grated Parmesan cheese and sea salt for topping, to taste

Mix together first 3 ingredients in a medium-sized glass bowl and microwave on high for 1½ minutes, stirring every 30 seconds.

Add the remaining ingredients and mix together with a mixer. Set aside in a warm place to rise for 30 minutes. The mixture will be fairly runny.

Preheat oven to 450 F.

Pour a thin layer of the mixture onto a parchment paper-lined pizza pan or pour smaller circles of dough onto parchment paper-lined cookie sheets (make the circles the size of the pita circles you wish to make) and top with grated Parmesan cheese and sea salt.

Bake for at least 10 – 12 minutes, or until the cheese is golden brown all over the pitas.

PUMPKIN BREAD

I'm one of those people who loves autumn because it means I can put pumpkin in everything I cook, and no one will question my sanity! With canned pumpkin available year-round though, there is really no excuse not to make this bread any time of year. It is moist and flavorful, and best of all, low fat. Although I have another pumpkin muffin recipe, this one can also be made as muffins.

¾ cup canned pumpkin
1 egg
¾ cup light brown sugar
⅛ cup oil or oil substitute
¼ cup evaporated milk (light is okay)
1 ¼ cup Nearly Normal Gluten-Free Flour Mix™
¼ tsp. baking soda
1 Tbs. baking powder
pinch of salt
1 Tbs. pumpkin pie spice
¼ tsp. cloves
¼ cup raisins or dried cranberries (optional)
¼ cup nuts (optional)

Preheat oven to 350 F.

Mix pumpkin, egg, sugar, oil and milk until smooth. Add Nearly Normal Gluten-Free Flour Mix™, baking soda, baking powder, salt and spices, and beat until well mixed. Stir in optional ingredients, if desired.

Pour batter into a greased bread pan and bake for approximately 40 minutes until the edges are browning and a cake·tester or toothpick inserted into the center of the bread is clean. Cool in the pan for 5 – 10 minutes and invert to remove, placing on a cooling rack until ready to serve.

Nearly Normal Cooking™ for Gluten-Free Eating

PUMPKIN MUFFINS

This recipe yields light and moist muffins that are great for snacking on in the cool autumn months. The recipe is easy to whip together for a quick breakfast solution too!

¼ cup shortening
½ cup light brown sugar
1 ¼ cup Nearly Normal Gluten-Free Flour Mix™
½ cup milk
¾ cup canned pumpkin
1 egg
1 Tbs. baking powder
¼ tsp. baking soda
pinch of salt
1 Tbs. pumpkin pie spice
¼ cup raisins or dried cranberries (optional)
¼ cup nuts (optional)
cinnamon sugar mixture (3 Tbs. sugar + ½ tsp. cinnamon)

Preheat oven to 350 F.

Blend shortening and sugar until fluffy. Add the egg, pumpkin and dry ingredients alternating with milk and mixing well. Stir in optional ingredients, if desired. Scoop into greased or paper-lined muffin tins and sprinkle cinnamon sugar mixture over the tops before baking. Bake for 18 minutes, or until the muffins have become lightly browned, fluffy and solid.

Makes 10 – 12 muffins.

SCONES/SHORTCAKES

My husband is my barometer for all my baking; he smells these cooking and grabs a handful before heading out the door for work, so I know that they're a hit. I have shared this recipe with a few select friends, and they report that their non-gluten-free guests always ask for the recipe — another good sign! The recipe produces a light, semi-sweet scone that does not crumble and is good on its own for breakfast or tea, or in milk or berries for a shortcake-type dessert. As with many of my baking recipes, yogurt is used for moistness, but it shouldn't be overlooked for flavor. There is no reason to use plain yogurt in a baking recipe! Take advantage of the opportunity to liven up your creations by experimenting with yogurt flavors. One I particularly like is piña colada flavored yogurt. Even though I usually add frozen berries to my scones, the piña colada kick, with a few pineapples thrown in, adds a lot to the recipe.

2 cups Nearly Normal Gluten-Free Flour Mix™
¼ cup sugar
2 tsp. baking powder
½ tsp. baking soda
4 Tbs. shortening
2 large eggs (mixed) or egg substitute
¾ cup (6 oz.) yogurt
frozen berries; raisins; orange rind; nuts; etc. optional for shortcakes
cinnamon sugar mixture (3 Tbs. sugar + ½ tsp. cinnamon)

Preheat oven to 400 F.

Mix together all dry ingredients in a large bowl. Cut shortening into dry ingredients using a pastry cutter or two knives. Add mixed eggs and yogurt.

If making scones, add to final mixture any berries, nuts or raisins. Scoop heaping tablespoonfuls onto a baking sheet lined with parchment paper* and bake for 10 – 12 minutes, until the tops are lightly browned. Do not overcook!

If making shortcakes, roll out onto a surface dusted with cornstarch to a thickness of about ¾ inch. Cut into circles or other shapes with cookie cutters. Place onto a greased cookie sheet and brush the tops with butter or non-dairy substitute and sprinkle with a pre-made cinnamon and sugar mixture. Bake for 8 – 10 minutes, just until the tops are lightly browned. Do not overcook!

*BAKING TIP: Lining a baking sheet with parchment paper is particularly helpful when you are baking with berries. The berries in these scones, for example, tend to stick and burn to a greased baking sheet, but they do not overcook or stick when using parchment paper.

SOUR CREAM MUFFINS

This cinnamon-y muffins make great individual coffee cakes.

¼ cup shortening
½ cup sugar
1 cup sour cream
1 ¼ cup Nearly Normal Gluten-Free Flour Mix™
2 eggs
3 tsp. baking powder
¼ tsp. baking soda
½ tsp. salt
1 tsp. cinnamon or pumpkin pie spice

Topping:
3 Tbs. sugar
½ tsp. cinnamon

Preheat oven to 350 F.

Prepare at least 12 muffin pans by greasing them or lining them with muffin papers.

Combine the shortening and sugar, mixing until fluffy. Beat in the remaining ingredients until the batter is smooth and very thick.

Pour batter into the muffin pans about 2/3 full. Sprinkle the tops with the cinnamon-sugar topping. Cut through the tops with a toothpick in a criss-cross or swirl design to marbleize the muffins.

Bake for 20 minutes, or until a toothpick or cake tester inserted into the muffins is clean and the muffins are lightly browned.

SOUTHERN CORNBREAD

I love cornbread: with soup, with preserves or just out of the pan. So I looked long and hard for a recipe that was moist, a touch sweet (like the kind I grew up eating in the South) and not so crumbly as gluten-free cornbreads tend to be. I think this recipe meets those needs. Feel free to add more or less sugar to your own taste.

1 cup milk
1 egg
¼ cup yogurt
¼ tsp. apple cider vinegar
¾ cup Nearly Normal Gluten-Free Flour Mix™
1 tsp. salt
½ tsp. baking soda
1 Tbs. baking powder
¾ cup cornmeal
¾ cup sugar

Preheat oven to 375 F.

Mix the liquid ingredients then add other ingredients, mixing until the lumps are removed. The batter will be thin, but not watery. Pour the batter into a greased 8 x 8 baking pan or into greased or lined muffin pans. Bake for 30 minutes for the cornbread, less for the muffins, according to your oven. The bread will be done when the top is lightly browned and a cake tester or toothpick in the center of the bread is clean. Do not over cook!

Nearly Normal Cooking™ for Gluten-Free Eating

ZUCCHINI BREAD

When I was in graduate school, I used to bake muffins, breads and cookies as a way to relieve stress. I started selling these at the university's café when my stress grew to such levels that I could no longer just give away all the produce of my labor to my hungry friends. One of the favorites of the café crowd was my zucchini bread. So, when I was diagnosed with celiac disease, it was one of the first recipes I tried to convert to gluten-free. It is also one that proved elusive until recently. Most recipes out there use an abundance of oil and are too heavy. With most gluten-free flours, this means that the middle of the bread will not cook through. My recipe has lots of loft, has the bonus of being low in fat and is great as muffins or bread. During the summer months, I will buy extra zucchini, grate it and freeze it in 2 cup measurements so that we can enjoy this quick bread year-round. It is now the only way I can get my son to eat a green vegetable!

3 eggs
2 cups sugar
½ cup oil or oil substitute
1 tsp. vanilla extract
3 cups Nearly Normal Gluten-Free Flour Mix™
3 tsp. cinnamon
3 tsp. baking powder
1 tsp. baking soda
2 cups fresh grated zucchini
½ cup nuts (optional)

Preheat oven to 350 F.

Beat the eggs until foamy, adding sugar and oil substitute until well blended. Add the sifted dry ingredients. Fold in the grated zucchini until well blended. Add nuts.

If baking as a loaf, grease two large loaf pans and fill each ½ full. Bake for approximately 1 hour and 10 minutes, testing to be sure the middle is cooked through. If your oven cooks the tops of these loaves too quickly, cover with aluminum foil to prevent burning. If you want to use this as a breakfast bread, you can sprinkle the tops with Confectioner's sugar.

If baking as muffins, grease and ½ fill 24 muffin tins. Bake for approximately 30 minutes, testing to be sure the middle is cooked through.

Desserts

APPLE-BERRY CRUMBLE

This recipe is always a favorite in the summer when there are plenty of fresh fruits available; however, I have made it with frozen berries as well. Feel free to substitute the fruits in this crumble, but if you're exclusively using juicy fruits like berries, it works best if you mix 1 tablespoon of cornstarch into the fruit mixture before baking.

Fruit:
2-3 baking apples, peeled and sliced thinly
1 cup blueberries, blackberries or raspberries, washed
1 tsp. lemon juice
3 Tbs. brown sugar
½ tsp. vanilla

Crumble:
1 cup Nearly Normal Gluten-Free Flour Mix™
1 pinch of salt
1 tsp. cinnamon or pumpkin pie spice
½ cup chopped pecans (optional)
4 Tbs. butter, margarine or shortening
2 Tbs. buttermilk

Preheat oven to 375 F.

Mix together all fruit ingredients in a separate bowl and set aside. In a mixing bowl, sift together all dry ingredients, then add butter in small chunks. Mix together until it is crumbly. Slowly add the buttermilk until the mixture is lumpy.

Arrange the fruit mixture on the bottom of an 8 x 8 baking dish or casserole. Top with the crumble mixture and cover tightly with foil. Bake for 25 minutes. Remove the foil and crisp for 5-10 minutes more, or until the topping is slightly browned.

Serve warm with vanilla ice cream or yogurt.

Nearly Normal Cooking™ for Gluten-Free Eating

ANGEL FOOD CAKE

This recipe is truly "Nearly Normal" and totally delicious!

6 eggs, separated
1 ½ cups sugar
1 ½ tsp. grated lemon or orange rind (optional)
2 Tbs. lemon or orange juice
1 ¼ cups potato starch
¼ cup boiling water

Preheat oven to 300 F.

Separate eggs, beating the whites until stiff peaks form, then set that bowl aside.
Place the yolks in a large bowl and mix until light. Gradually mix the sugar in with
the yolks. Add rind and juice to the boiling water, then mix in with the egg yolk
mixture until totally blended. Fold in the potato starch, then gently fold in the beaten
egg whites.

Pour the batter gently into an ungreased 10-inch tube pan or spring form pan. Bake
for 30 minutes, then increase the heat to 350 F and bake 40 minutes longer. Invert
the pan and allow to cool before removing the cake. Top with your favorite fresh
fruit.

BANANA CAKE

Living in Florida spoils you for living anywhere else where fresh fruit is hard to come by year round. Now that I live outside of the Sunshine State, I relish all recipes that incorporate readily obtainable fresh fruit. This cake recipe works particularly well gluten-free — it is moist, flavorful and best of all, uses fresh fruit. I've included a recipe for banana frosting, but I also like a cream cheese icing (pg. 105) with this cake and I have even baked it as a birthday cake with plain white icing.

3 cups Nearly Normal Gluten-Free Flour Mix™
1 tsp. baking soda
2 tsp. baking powder
1 tsp. guar gum
¾ cup margarine or vegetable shortening
2 ¼ cups sugar
3 eggs, well beaten
5 ripe bananas, mashed
¼ cup buttermilk
2 tsp. vanilla extract
1 cup finely chopped pecans (optional)

Preheat oven to 325 F.

Grease and "flour" with cornstarch three 9-inch round cake pans. Combine the dry ingredients and set aside. Cream together the butter and sugar until smooth. Pour in the eggs and mix well. Stir in the bananas and add the dry ingredients and buttermilk, alternating between the two. Stir in the vanilla extract and pecans last.

Divide the batter between the three pans and bake for 25 minutes, or until the edges pull away from the sides of the pans or a cake tester inserted into the center of each cake comes out clean. Remove from the oven and allow to cool for at least 5 minutes before turning onto racks to cool.

BANANA FROSTING & FILLING

½ cup mashed bananas (approximately 2 bananas)
2 tsp. fresh lemon juice
½ cup (1 stick) margarine or butter at room temperature (not melted!)
1 box (1 lb) Confectioner's sugar
1 tsp. vanilla extract
3 ripe bananas sliced thinly

In a small bowl, mix the mashed bananas and the lemon juice together and set aside. In another bowl, cream together the butter and sugar with an electric mixer. Add the mashed bananas, blending well and stir in the vanilla extract.

Spread a layer of icing on one of the cooled cake rounds, then top with a layer of sliced bananas. Place the second cake layer on top of the bananas and repeat the layers. After placing the third layer on top, smooth icing over the sides and top of the cake.

BREAKFAST CAKE

My son says this is the "best kind of cake ever" – probably because I let him eat this cake for breakfast! It actually does make a nice light coffee cake-like dish that rarely lasts past breakfast. The fragrant smell of the butter and cinnamon baking early in the morning guarantees that your family or house guests will be eager to finish this cake off in a hurry.

1 egg
¼ cup oil or oil substitute
¼ cup vanilla yogurt
¼ cup sugar
1 ½ cups Nearly Normal Gluten-Free Flour Mix™
¼ tsp. baking soda
1 Tbs. baking powder
½ tsp. cinnamon
2/3 cup milk (skim works fine)
½ tsp. salt
1 tsp. vanilla extract

Topping:
½ tsp. cinnamon or pumpkin pie spice
3 Tbs. sugar
2 Tbs. softened butter or margarine
1 large apple, sliced

Preheat oven to 350 F.

Grease an 8 x 8 baking dish and set aside. In a medium-sized bowl, combine all cake ingredients and mix until the batter is smooth. Pour into the prepared baking dish. In a small bowl, combine the topping ingredients, then pour over the cake batter. Cut through the topping with a knife pointed down making criss-cross or circular patterns in the top of the cake to marbleize the cake. Lay apple slices across the top of the marbleized cake.

Bake for 40 minutes, or until a cake tester or toothpick inserted in the middle of the cake comes out clean.

BROWNIES

This is a good old fashioned brownie recipe to which you may add chocolate or peanut butter chips or nuts, and onto which you may spread icing, Confectioner's sugar or sprinkles to dress them up for special occasions!

½ cup shortening or oil
1 ⅓ cups sugar
3 eggs
2 tsp. vanilla extract
1 ¼ cup Nearly Normal Gluten-Free Flour Mix
¾ cup cocoa
2 tsp. baking powder
1 tsp. guar gum
½ tsp. salt
1 cup milk

Preheat oven to 350 F.

Grease a 9 x 13 baking pan and set aside.
In a large bowl, cream together the sugar and shortening or oil until fluffy. Add the eggs and vanilla extract, mixing well. Add the remaining ingredients in the order listed above, mixing until smooth.

Pour the batter into the prepared pan and bake for approximately 20 minutes, or until a toothpick or cake tester inserted into the center of the pan comes out clean.

CARROT CAKE

Carrot cake has long been a favorite in my family – my husband even chose it as his groom's cake at our rehearsal dinner! So, devising a gluten-free version has been a top priority for me! This recipe uses lots of alternative ingredients to create that moist flavorful cake we all love. The result is an amazingly low-fat gluten-free copy of the traditional recipe that was very heavy on the oil. Enjoy!

2 cups grated carrots, packed
½ cup raisins (preferably baking raisins)
9 oz. crushed unsweetened pineapple, undrained
½ cup sugar
2 ¼ cups Nearly Normal Gluten-Free Flour Mix™
2 tsp. baking soda
2 tsp. cinnamon
1 tsp. nutmeg

½ cup shredded coconut
3 eggs
¼ cup honey
¼ cup oil
¼ cup vanilla yogurt
1 tsp. baking powder
1 tsp. ginger

Preheat oven to 325 F.

In a large bowl, combine the carrots, coconut, undrained pineapple and raisins. In a separate bowl, beat the eggs until they are light. Add the honey and sugar until the mixture is frothy. Add the oil and yogurt and blend. Pour this egg mixture into the larger bowl with the carrot mixture. Stir, then add the dry ingredients. Beat until thoroughly mixed.

Pour the batter into a greased 9 x 13 cake pan. Bake for 45 minutes, or until a cake tester inserted into the center of the cake comes out clean. Let the cake cool for at least 10 minutes if you intend to remove it from the pan to frost it.

CREAM CHEESE FROSTING

No carrot cake would be complete without a cream cheese frosting! You may use lowfat cream cheese, but the frosting will not be as thick.

1 (8 oz) package of cream cheese, softened slightly
½ cup butter or margarine, softened slightly
2 cups powdered sugar
1 tsp. vanilla
1 cup finely chopped pecans (optional)

Combine the cream cheese and butter, beating until it is smooth. Add the powdered sugar and the vanilla and beat together until the frosting is light and fluffy. Add the nuts, if you choose. This recipe makes about 3 cups of frosting.

Nearly Normal Cooking™ for Gluten-Free Eating

CHERRY ONE EGG CAKE

This recipe dates back at least to the cookbooks of my great-grandmother's day, and is my husband's favorite childhood dessert memory. My grandmother thankfully came across it in her own mother's recipes after my husband and I had searched for years for his mother's recipe for fruit "cobbler." While hardly a cobbler, the fruit addition is essential and makes this cake light and scrumptious.

2 cups Nearly Normal Gluten-Free Flour Mix™
4 tsp. baking powder
¼ tsp. salt
4 Tbs. butter or shortening
1 cup sugar
1 egg, unbeaten
¾ cup milk
1 tsp. vanilla extract
1 jar of tart cherries

Preheat oven to 350 F.

Mix all dry ingredients thoroughly and add to mixed butter, egg, milk and vanilla extract gradually. Stir cherries in gently before pouring mixture into a greased 8 x 8 baking pan. Bake for 50 minutes, or until it tests done in the center and is lightly browned.

Some folks like this recipe served with milk poured over it in a dish, or with vanilla ice cream, but it is truly delicious on its own.

CHOCOLATE CANDY

You can shape these chocolates into any size and shape. Get creative for Easter eggs, Valentine's hearts, Halloween pumpkins.... Change the flavor to this base recipe by adding approximately 2 cups of peanut butter, cocoa or coconut.

1 lb. butter (at room temperature)
4 lb. Confectioner's sugar
½ cup mashed potato flakes
Commercially prepared chocolate candy melts (bitter-dark chocolate)*

Line baking sheets with waxed paper and set aside.

Combine all ingredients in a large bowl by squishing together with your hands until mixed through. Shape the mixture as you wish and place on waxed paper on a cookie sheet. Set overnight, if possible, in a cool place.

Prepare the chocolate candy melts by heating on a stove and dipping the chocolate candy according to package directions. Set back on the waxed paper to cool.

*BAKING TIP: If you do not have chocolate candy melts, the chocolate recipes for Chocolate-Dipped Strawberries on page 111 work nicely too!

Nearly Normal Cooking™ for Gluten-Free Eating

CHOCOLATE CHIP COOKIES I

This recipe will seem a lot like the traditional one you are used to making — why change an old favorite? When creating this recipe, I modified only where necessary to make a gluten-free version. Luckily, Nearly Normal Gluten-Free Flour Mix™ performs so much like regular wheat flour that very few changes had to be made. Enjoy!

¼ lb. (1 stick) butter
¼ lb. (1 stick) shortening
1 cup firmly packed brown sugar
½ cup granulated sugar
1 tsp. salt
2 tsp. vanilla extract
2 large eggs
1 tsp. baking soda
½ tsp. baking powder
2 ¼ cups Nearly Normal Gluten-Free Flour Mix™
12 oz. semi-sweet chocolate chips, peanut butter chips, butterscotch chips or a mixture thereof
1 ½ cups chopped pecans (optional)

Preheat oven to 350 F.

Bring the butter and shortening to room temperature, then beat together until creamy. Add sugars, salt and vanilla extract, mixing until fluffy. Beat in eggs, baking soda and baking powder, then add the Nearly Normal Gluten-Free Flour Mix™. Stir in chips and nuts, if so desired. Drop by measured teaspoonful onto a greased cookie sheet, at least 1 inch apart. Bake for 9-12 minutes, or until the tops are lightly browned. Let them stand 5 minutes before removing them to cooling racks.

CHOCOLATE CHIP COOKIES II

This recipe is an interesting variation on an old stand-by recipe, as it includes rice bran among its ingredients. Hey – it's almost healthy! It makes a crunchy cookie, so be sure not to overcook. This recipe is also good without the chips, but with heaps of colorful sprinkles on top instead (the method preferred by my preschooler).

2 eggs
2/3 cup shortening
1/3 cup vanilla yogurt
3/4 cup white sugar
1/4 cup light brown sugar, firmly packed
1 tsp. vanilla extract
1 1/4 cups Nearly Normal Gluten-Free Flour Mix™
1/4 cup rice bran
3 Tbs. potato starch
1/2 tsp. baking soda
dash of salt
3/4 cups semi-sweet chocolate chips (optional)
1/2 cup chopped nuts (optional)

Preheat oven to 350 F.

Cream shortening, yogurt and sugars, then add eggs and vanilla extract. Mix together dry ingredients and then add to the creamed mixture. If using, stir in chips and nuts. Drop by measured teaspoon onto greased cookie sheets (at this point add the sprinkles if your child insists) and bake for 15 minutes, or until the edges are lightly browned.

CHOCOLATE-DIPPED STRAWBERRIES

For a sexy, festive or just plain delicious treat, you have got to try these!!! I've provided two options to try, depending on the ingredients you have on hand.

Recipe #1:
2 cups water
6 oz. bittersweet chocolate, chopped
3 Tbs. heavy cream
2 Tbs. butter
1 tsp. vanilla extract
1 lb. large strawberries with stems, washed and dried well
$1/3$ cup coconut, chopped pistachios or crushed gluten-free cookies (optional)

Recipe #2:
2 cups water
8 oz. semi-sweet chocolate chips
1 lb. large strawberries with stems, washed and dried well
$1/3$ cup coconut, chopped pistachios or crushed gluten-free cookies (optional)

Pour water into a pot and set onto the stovetop on medium-high heat. Place a heatproof bowl on top of the pot (not touching the water) to create a double-boiler.

Add the chocolate and melt.
(If using recipe #1, also add heavy cream, butter and vanilla extract and whisk together).

Dip the strawberries into the mixture one at a time, then twirl to shake off the excess chocolate. Set on a wax paper-covered cookie sheet or tray and refrigerate for at least 30 minutes until set. Do not refrigerate for longer than one hour though, as condensation will form on the chocolate). As an added touch, 5 seconds after you dipped the strawberries in the chocolate you can dip them in crushed gluten-free cookies, nuts or coconut.

CORNMEAL SHORTCAKES

This is a nice alternative to the scones/shortcakes recipe on page 94. It can be served with any kind of fresh berries, or warmed with ice cream!

5 Tbs. butter or margarine at room temperature
¼ cup vanilla yogurt
¾ cup Nearly Normal Gluten-Free Flour Mix™
½ cup almond flour
½ cup cornmeal
¾ cup sugar
¼ tsp. salt
dash of baking soda
2 eggs
1 tsp. vanilla extract
cinnamon sugar mixture (3 Tbs. sugar + ½ tsp. cinnamon) (optional)
sliced almonds (optional)

Preheat oven to 350 F.

In a medium-sized bowl, cream the sugar and butter together until fluffy. Add the eggs, vanilla and salt and mix until the consistency looks curdled. Add the yogurt, Nearly Normal Gluten-Free Flour Mix™, almond flour and cornmeal as well as the baking soda. Mix until smooth and light.

Spoon batter into muffin tins prepared with butter or non-stick spray and sprinkled with cornstarch. Top with cinnamon-sugar or sliced almonds.

This recipe makes approximately 12 regular-sized shortcakes or 6 large shortcakes (if using jumbo muffin tins). Bake until lightly browned, approximately 20 – 25 minutes.

Serve warm by cutting each shortcake in half and spooning berries or ice cream in between each half and over the tops.

Nearly Normal Cooking™ for Gluten-Free Eating

CRÊPES

This recipe tastes exactly like the real thing straight from the crêperies at Sacré-Coeur on the top of Montmartre! Use your imagination to create fillings with seasonal berries, chocolate, cinnamon-sugar or other combinations. Or, if you are brave, you could try the famous French or Belgian Crêpe Suzette, which is served with lightly grated orange peel and liqueur (usually Grand Marnier) and is lit before serving!

2 Tbs. Nearly Normal Gluten-Free Flour Mix™
3 eggs, slightly beaten
3 Tbs. milk
½ tsp. salt
½ tsp. vanilla extract
Confectioner's sugar
Fresh berries or other filling of your choice

Prepare a small frying pan by heating it to medium-low heat and then adding one tablespoon of butter or margarine.

Combine all the crêpe ingredients in a small bowl, mixing until there are no lumps.

When the butter has melted, pour a thin layer of batter onto the pan. Pick up the pan and move it around until all the batter spreads out thinly and begins to set. Cook for only about one minute, or until the batter is completely set on the bottom. Flip the crêpe over gently and cook for only a half of a minute on the other side. Do not burn! Set crêpe aside, cover and repeat until all batter is used.

Sprinkle the inside of each crêpe with your chosen filling, such as Confectioner's sugar and fresh berries. Then wrap the crêpe over itself and lay each rolled crêpe on a plate. Serve warm.

DEATH BY (FLOURLESS) CHOCOLATE CAKE

This decadent chocolate cake is so sinfully rich that no one will ever miss the flour! Try serving it with whipped or ice cream and a sprinkle of fresh berries.

1 lb. semi-sweet chocolate
1 Tbs. vanilla extract
1 Tbs. rum
¾ cup strong black coffee
8 eggs
½ cup granulated sugar
¾ cup heavy cream
Whipped or ice cream and berries for garnish (optional)

Preheat oven to 300 F.

Butter a 10-inch cake pan and refrigerate until ready to use. Also have ready a double boiler or a glass or metal bowl and slightly larger pot for use on the stove, another larger mixing bowl, a medium sized mixing bowl, a small mixing bowl and a roasting pan.

Break up the chocolate into small pieces and place in a bowl or double boiler. Add vanilla extract, rum and pre-made coffee. Set the bowl over a pan of simmering water to melt chocolate, stirring occasionally to remove any lumps. Remove from the heat as soon as the chocolate has melted and transfer mixture to a large mixing bowl to cool. In a medium bowl, whisk together the eggs and sugar until thick then beat in about a quarter of the cooled chocolate mixture. Pour this mixture into the remaining chocolate mixture and blend gently. With a mixer, whip the heavy cream in a small mixing bowl until it forms soft peaks; fold into the chocolate/egg mixture with a spatula just until it is combined. Pour the batter into the prepared cake pan and place it inside a deep roasting pan. Pour enough boiling water into the roaster to come halfway up the sides of the cake pan. Bake for one hour.

Remove cake pan from the oven and let it cool to room temperature. Chill in the refrigerator overnight.

To serve, remove the cake from the pan and cover the top with whipped or ice cream and sprinkled berries.

Nearly Normal Cooking™ for Gluten-Free Eating

FAMILY FUDGE

My mother has been making this recipe since I was a little girl and she has modified it to fit modern kitchens by creating a microwave version (which is much easier!). Variations you may want to try include adding nuts, substituting peanut butter chips for chocolate chips or topping with crushed candy canes or colored sprinkles.

3 cups sugar
1 ½ sticks butter or margarine
5 oz. evaporated milk (may use fat free)
12 oz. semi-sweet chocolate chips
1 jar marshmallow crème
1 tsp. vanilla extract
1 cup chopped nuts (optional)

Place sugar, butter and evaporated milk in a large microwave-safe bowl and microwave on high heat until melted. With a wooden spoon, stir, then microwave until the mixture comes to a full rolling boil. At this point, without turning the microwave off or opening the door, add 5 minutes of boiling time to the mixture.

Meanwhile, grease a 9 x 13 baking pan. Open the jar of marshmallow crème and the bag of chocolate chips so that they are ready to add immediately after the boiling process.

Pour the chips and scoop the marshmallow crème into the boiling mixture and stir vigorously to mix. Add vanilla extract and nuts, if you choose, then use a mixer to beat the mixture until smooth. Quickly pour into the prepared pan and smooth using a rubber spatula. Add any toppings you desire at this point, then set aside to cool. Do not cut until the fudge has cooled.

FAVORITE CUT-OUT COOKIES

I sought to devise a workable, tasty cut-out cookie recipe for a long time, and this one is great! It is easy to roll and cut, resilient, elastic and yummy. One afternoon I made the recipe for a play date and the kids rolled and cut the cookies, decorated and baked them. One of the other mothers commented that she couldn't believe how many times we rolled the dough out to cut all the cookies (kids aren't the most efficient cookie cutters!). The dough never got crumbly or hard like her recipe (with gluten), so she wanted my recipe! It is good to double this recipe if you want to have enough to share!

¼ cup shortening
¼ cup oil
⅔ cup sugar
2 egg yolks
2 tsp. vanilla extract
1 ¾ cup Nearly Normal Gluten-Free Flour Mix™
½ tsp. salt
3 Tbs. water (as needed)
food coloring

Preheat oven to 350 F.

Cream shortening, sugar and oil until fluffy. Add separated egg yolks, vanilla extract and food coloring. Add in Nearly Normal Gluten-Free Flour Mix™ and salt, alternating with water as necessary to achieve the desired consistency. Refrigerate for at least one hour, if possible.

Lightly flour the rolling surface and rolling pin with Nearly Normal Gluten-Free Flour Mix™ or cornstarch. Roll the dough to approximately ⅛ inch thickness and dust cookie cutters before using to cut shapes.

Place cookies onto a greased cookie sheet and decorate with sprinkles, if desired. Bake approximately 8-10 minutes until they begin to lightly brown at the edges. When baked, frost with gluten-free icing, if desired.

Nearly Normal Cooking™ for Gluten-Free Eating

FLOURLESS COOKIES

These treats are fun to make for a different kind of sweet. No flour, no baking, and they are almost good for you!

¼ lb. (1 stick) margarine or butter
1 cup sugar
1 egg
1 cup finely chopped dates
1 cup finely chopped pecans
2 cups gluten-free crispy rice cereal
1 tsp. vanilla extract
1 cup +/- coconut, to taste

Combine margarine, sugar, egg and dates in a medium saucepan over medium heat.

Let the ingredients come to a boil and lower the heat, cooking for an additional one minute. Remove from heat and add vanilla extract. Stir in nuts and crispy rice cereal. Let the mixture sit until it is cool enough to handle, but not yet solid.

Sprinkle coconut over wax paper while cooling. Roll teaspoon-sized cookies in your hands and in the coconut. Place cookies on a plate to fully cool.

No baking necessary!

FRUIT COBBLER

This cobbler is an easy summertime favorite devised by my mother some years ago and modified only slightly to render it gluten-free. Peaches, or any kind of summer berry make it delicious, but even a winter craving may be satisfied by using frozen berries.

Filling:
Peeled and sliced fruit of your choice, enough to thickly cover the bottom of an 8 x 8
        square baking pan
1 tsp. lemon juice (if using peaches, nectarines or similar fruit)
½ – 1 cup sugar
cinnamon to taste
¼ cup cornstarch

Topping:
1 cup Nearly Normal Gluten-Free Flour Mix™
1 cup sugar
1 egg, beaten
cinnamon to taste
¼ cup melted margarine or butter

Preheat oven to 350 F.

Layer fruit in bottom of baking pan and sprinkle with lemon juice, if necessary. Next sprinkle the sugar, cinnamon and cornstarch. Combine the Nearly Normal Gluten-Free Flour Mix™ with sugar and cinnamon, then add the egg. Stir until crumbly, then sprinkle over the fruit. Pour melted margarine over cobbler and bake for 30 minutes. This dessert is especially good served warm with vanilla ice cream!

FORGOTTEN COOKIES

This recipe is a great one to make and leave in the oven overnight for an event the next day. Not only are there hardly any ingredients, there is hardly any effort in these cookies – it's the best kind of recipe!

2 egg whites
¼ tsp. salt
¾ cup sugar
½ cup black walnuts or 12 oz. package chocolate chips

Preheat oven to 375 F.

Beat egg whites and salt until stiff. Add sugar gradually, also beating until stiff. Fold in nuts or chips. Drop by teaspoonfuls onto greased cookie sheet. Place in the oven and turn the oven off immediately! Do not open the oven for at least 4 hours ... "forget" about them!

FRENCH SUNKEN CHOCOLATE CAKE

My dear neighbor kindly prepares this cake whenever they have my husband and me over for dinner. The fact that there are only 3 tablespoons of flour makes it possible to modify this recipe easily without any noticeable difference in consistency or flavor. She has modified it with almond flour, but it works just as well with Nearly Normal Gluten-Free Flour Mix™; it is a guaranteed neighbor-pleaser!

10 oz. bittersweet chocolate (or .63 lb)
1 cup butter
5 large eggs
1 ¼ cups sugar
3 Tbs. Nearly Normal Gluten-Free Flour Mix™ or almond flour
1 ½ tsp. baking powder
Confectioner's sugar for topping

Preheat oven to 325 F.

Butter and "flour" with cornstarch a 10" spring form pan.
Place the butter and chocolate into a saucepan over low-medium heat and stir until the mixture is smooth.

Beat the eggs separately then add the sugar until well-blended and beginning to thicken. Gradually add the Nearly Normal Gluten-Free Flour Mix™ and baking powder. Gently fold in the chocolate mixture then transfer the batter to the prepared pan.

Bake uncovered for 20 minutes, then cover with foil and continue to bake for 40 additional minutes, or until a cake tester comes out with moist crumbs attached. Uncover the cake and cool in the pan on a rack. Remove the form and sift Confectioner's sugar over the top of the cake before serving. This recipe is also heavenly when served warm with vanilla ice cream!

GINGERSNAPS

I have tried my share of gluten-free gingersnap recipes but I return again and again to my family's recipe, modified only slightly by the substitution of Nearly Normal Gluten-Free Flour Mix™. This is one of those recipes that everyone says tastes "like a real cookie!"

1 cup shortening
½ cup margarine or butter
2 cups sugar
2 eggs
½ cup dark molasses
4 cups Nearly Normal Gluten-Free Flour Mix™
2 tsp. baking soda
2 tsp. cloves
1 Tbs. cinnamon
2 tsp. ginger

Preheat oven to 350 F.

Mix shortening, margarine and sugar together until fluffy. Beat in the eggs and molasses thoroughly. Mix the dry ingredients and add to the creamed batter. Roll pieces of dough into 1 inch balls and roll in sugar. Place on greased cookie sheets and bake for approximately 10 minutes — longer if you prefer a crispier cookie.

GRAHAM-LIKE CRACKERS

Some non-gluten-free friends of mine refer to these crackers as "American Biscotti" as they dip them in their coffee. However you choose to use these versatile crackers, they're sure to be a hit, because this cookie not only tastes good by itself, but it also makes a fantastic graham-like cracker crust and wonderful s'mores! Sprinkle sugar and cinnamon on top before baking for variety, or substitute molasses for the honey and add 2 tsp. ginger and 1 tsp. cloves to the dough to make these crackers taste like crispy gingersnaps!

¾ cup butter or shortening
¼ cup honey
1 cup brown sugar
1 tsp. vanilla extract
1 ½ cups Nearly Normal Gluten-Free Flour Mix™
1 cup rice flour
½ cup buckwheat or brown rice flour
dash of salt
2 tsp. cinnamon
3 tsp. baking powder
½ cup water

Beat together the first four ingredients in one large bowl and mix all of the remaining ingredients except the water in another bowl. Slowly stir the dry mixture into the first bowl, adding water as necessary to create a consistency such that you could make a ball with the dough. Divide the dough in half and refrigerate for one hour or more.

Preheat oven to 325 F.

Roll one half out onto a surface "floured" with cornstarch. The dough should make a large ¼ inch thick rectangle. You may roll it more thinly or more thickly, depending on how you prefer your crackers: the thinner the dough, the crispier the cracker. Cut into smaller rectangles like graham crackers and lift with a "floured" spatula onto a greased baking sheet. Finally, prick each cracker with a fork in rows, as you would with a graham cracker.

Bake for 25 – 30 minutes, or until they are lightly browned. Let cool on the baking sheet 5 minutes before transferring to a cooling rack.

Nearly Normal Cooking™ for Gluten-Free Eating

GRAND MARNIER CHEESECAKE

This cheesecake is more like a cake than any other cheesecake I've tried. It is truly dreamy, with a surprisingly welcome crunchy touch. The addition of the Grand Marnier, while not necessary, completes the fresh orange flavor of this cake, and is as decadent as it is delicious!

Crust:
1 ½ cups Graham-Like Cracker crumbs (see page 122)
                    or commercial gluten-free rice bran or gingersnap cookies
4 Tbs. melted butter or margarine
¼ cup sugar

Cake:
1 ½ lb. cream cheese, softened
¼ cup heavy whipping cream
4 eggs
1 cup sugar
1 cup chopped mandarin oranges, with juice
1 tsp. vanilla
½ cup chopped pecans
2 Tbs. Grand Marnier

Preheat oven to 300 F.

Mix all crust ingredients together and press into the bottom of a pie pan. Refrigerate.

In a large bowl, mix together the cream cheese and heavy whipping cream until smooth. Add the eggs, one at a time, mixing completely between each addition. Add the sugar and finally, fold in the oranges, juice, Grand Marnier, vanilla and pecans. Pour the batter into the refrigerated, prepared crust. Bake for 1 hour or until it is firm to the touch.

GRANDMA'S PIE CRUST

I had just about given up on ever making a homemade pie after dropping yet another crumbly mess posing for a gluten-free pie crust all over the kitchen floor. Then, inspiration struck: what if, instead of trying all those expensive gluten-free pie crust mixes, or all the other 8+ ingredient GF recipes (purporting to be the absolute best gluten-free pie crust ever), I instead just used Nearly Normal Gluten-Free Flour Mix™ in my grandma's tried and true flaky pie crust? It was worth a try before I completely threw in the towel on ever making or enjoying pie again. Low and behold, when I made this simple 4 ingredient crust and was able to transfer it into the pie plate, shape it into an attractive crust and even serve it to others cheerfully, I knew I had found the elusive holy grail of GF pie crusts! Enjoy pies again with this easy to make and easy to shape crust that is also great for old-fashioned cinnamon rolls.

Makes one 8 or 9-inch pie crust (double for a two crust fruit pie)

1 cup Nearly Normal Gluten-Free Flour Mix™
½ tsp. salt
⅓ cup shortening
2 – 3 Tbs.+ cold water

Cut the mixture together using two knives or a pastry cutter. Add the water to make the consistency you need to form a ball. Refrigerate the dough for at least 15 minutes before rolling out onto a surface dusted with Nearly Normal Gluten-Free Flour Mix™ — I recommend a flexible pastry sheet or a large piece of plastic wrap on the counter for that purpose. Turn the pie plate upside-down on top of the rolled out crust and flip the crust and plate over. Pat into shape and fill with your desired filling. For a two-crust pie, gently flip the entire pastry sheet with rolled out pie crust over on top of the pie -- do not fold the crust in half to lay on top of the pie, or the crust will crack at the fold. Crimp the edges of the crust to form a scalloped edge. Put small pats of butter on top of the crust and sprinkle with cinnamon-sugar if you desire.

BERRY PIE

Add 4 cups of berries (or other diced fruit such as peaches, apples or pears), ½ cup of sugar and ¼ cup of Nearly Normal Gluten-Free Flour Mix™ together and pour into crust. Top with second crust and bake with the edges covered with foil at 375 F for 20 – 30 minutes. Remove the foil and bake another 10 – 20 minutes, just until the top is lightly browned.

CRISPY CINNAMON ROLLS

Roll the crust out onto a dusted pastry sheet. Spread butter or margarine over the entire crust. Sprinkle with cinnamon-sugar then cut the pastry into rows. Roll each roll up gently and place the cinnamon roll onto a greased cookie sheet. Bake at 350 F for 10 – 15 minutes, until the crusts begin to flake and are lightly browned.

HELLO DOLLIES

These bars have always been favorites in my household and happily, a quick substitution renders them gluten-free and still delicious!

1 stick margarine
1+ cup gluten-free graham crackers (see recipe pg. 122) or gingersnap cookies, crushed
1 cup coconut
1 cup chocolate chips
1 cup chopped nuts (optional)
1 can (15 oz.) sweetened condensed milk

Preheat oven to 350 F.

Melt butter in a 9 x 13 pan, either on the cooktop, in the oven, or if in a glass pan, in the microwave. Pour the crumbs into the pan on top of the melted butter, but do not stir. Layer the remaining ingredients in the following order: coconut; chocolate chips; nuts. Finally, pour the sweetened condensed milk over the bars in a lattice pattern. Ultimately, this will fill in over the whole pan.

Bake for 25 – 30 minutes, just until the milk has turned a light brown color.

HOT FUDGE PIE

I still remember burning my tongue on my mother's famous hot fudge pie as a child because I just couldn't wait to let it cool! This melt-in-your mouth (literally!) recipe was actually easily converted to a new gluten-free favorite. There is no difference in flavor between this recipe in its gluten-free or mainstream form — it's delicious!

½ cup cocoa
¾ cup boiling water
¼ lb (1 stick) margarine
1 cup sugar
⅓ cup Nearly Normal Gluten-Free Flour Mix™
2 eggs, separated
1 tsp. vanilla extract

Preheat oven 325 F.

Dissolve ½ cup cocoa in ¾ cup boiling water and set aside to cool. Cream the margarine with sugar, Nearly Normal Gluten-Free Flour Mix™, 2 separated egg yolks and vanilla extract. Add cooled chocolate mixture and fold in two stiffly beaten egg whites. Pour into a greased and floured (with cornstarch or Nearly Normal Gluten-Free Flour Mix™) 9-inch pie pan.

Bake for 1 hour and serve warm with vanilla ice cream, whipped cream or plain. Make sure it is not too hot when you eat it!

IMPOSSIBLE COCONUT PIE

This pie is another family favorite made gluten-free with only a few modifications. It is wonderful hot out of the oven, cold or even room temperature. I recommend doubling the recipe, because one pie is never enough!

4 eggs
1 ½ cups sugar
½ cup Nearly Normal Gluten-Free Flour Mix™
2 cups milk
1 tsp. vanilla extract
1 stick (8 Tbs.) melted butter or margarine
1 can flaked coconut, or 2 cups of bagged flaked coconut

Preheat oven to 350 F.

Pour coconut into a small bowl. Add milk to soak and set aside for at least 10 minutes. In a separate bowl, beat eggs and sugar and add all other ingredients slowly. Add the soaked coconut and pour into a greased pie pan. This pie rises when cooking, then shrinks as it cools; therefore, use caution not to overfill the pie pan. I recommend leaving an inch clearance to allow for the pie to rise. Consequently, you may find that you have extra pie batter and need to use an additional baking pan. This recipe also works well divided into several individual baking dishes to serve guests.

Bake for 50 – 60 minutes, or until the edges are lightly browned and the middle is no longer jiggly.

LEMON BARS

This recipe comes from a good friend who shares both my sweet tooth and the need for sweets to be made gluten-free. Everyone needs such a friend, because we keep each other inspired with new recipes like this one, which has become a holiday party favorite!

<u>Crust</u>
1/3 cup butter or margarine
1/4 cup sugar
1 cup Nearly Normal Gluten-Free Flour Mix™

<u>Filling</u>
2 eggs
3/4 cup sugar
2 Tbs. Nearly Normal Gluten-Free Flour Mix™
2 tsp. finely shredded lemon peel
3 Tbs. lemon juice
1/4 tsp. baking powder
Confectioner's sugar (optional)

Preheat oven to 350 F.

In a medium bowl, beat butter with a mixer on medium to high speed for 30 seconds. Add the sugar and beat until combined. Beat in the Nearly Normal Gluten Free Flour Mix™ until crumbly, being careful not to overmix. Press mixture into the bottom of an ungreased 8 x 8 baking pan. Bake for 15 minutes or until golden brown.

For filling, combine eggs, sugar, Nearly Normal Gluten-Free Flour Mix™, lemon peel, lemon juice and baking powder; beat until combined.

Pour filling over baked crust. Bake 20 minutes more or until set and lightly browned. Cool on a wire rack. Cut into bars when completely cool.

Makes 20 bars. This recipe doubles nicely when baked in a 9 x 13 pan.

LEMONADE PIE

This pie is a light, refreshing treat for hot summer afternoons.

<u>Filling</u>:
1 carton of whipped topping
2 small cans of lemonade or limeade
1 can sweetened condensed milk

<u>Crust</u>:
2 cups crushed gluten-free graham-like crackers or gingersnaps (see pp. 121-122)
2 Tbs. melted butter or margarine
2 Tbs. sugar

Preheat oven to 350 F.

Mix the crust ingredients and press into the bottom of a pie plate. Bake for 10 minutes, or until the crust has lightly browned. Allow to cool before mixing the filling.

Mix the filling ingredients together and beat until smooth. Pour into cooled pie crust and chill for at least one hour before serving.

MINI (& low fat) CHEESECAKES

These are great to bring to pot-luck dinners or to serve at your own party. You may top them with any combination of fresh fruit or gluten-free pie filling, whipped topping, cinnamon-sugar sprinkles or other garnish of your choice. Since they are both delicious and offer a somewhat guilt-free cheesecake option, don't expect to have any of these melt-in-your mouth treats left over!

1 envelope unflavored gelatin
½ cup sugar
1 cup boiling water
2 (8 oz.) pkgs. cream cheese, softened
1 tsp. vanilla or almond extract (depending on the topping you select)
1 large bag of gluten-free gingersnaps or graham-like crackers (see pg. 122)
Foil mini muffin liners.

Arrange mini foil muffin liners on a baking sheet with sides; make sure they are pressed together neatly, but tightly to give support when the batter is poured inside. Crumble the gingersnaps and sprinkle to cover the bottom of each of the muffin cups as a ¼ inch crust. You can do this in a food processor, blender or the old fashioned way — by placing the cookies in a large ziptop bag and running a rolling pin over the cookies until they reach the desired consistency.

In a small bowl, add boiling water to the sugar and gelatin and stir until completely dissolved (about 5 minutes).

In a separate large bowl, beat together the cream cheese and vanilla or almond extract until smooth. Slowly add in the gelatin mixture. Pour into the muffin liners.

Refrigerate for 3 hours or at least until firm. Add your preferred topping after the cheesecakes have set up.

OLDE WORLD APPLE PANCAKES

Pancakes aren't just for breakfast anymore! At least, these sweet treats may be served bright and early or really late. They can be baked as individual cakes by using jumbo muffin tins, or you can bake one large cake in a 10-inch nonstick ovenproof skillet or baking pan.

3 eggs, lightly beaten
1 Tbs. lemon juice
¾ cup milk
¼ cup light brown sugar
⅔ cup Nearly Normal Gluten-Free Flour Mix™
1 tsp. cinnamon
½ tsp. salt
4 Tbs. butter
2 large Granny Smith, Gala or Fuji apples, peeled and cut into pieces

Preheat oven to 400 F.

Peel, core and slice each apple into small wedges, then cut each wedge into approximately three pieces. Toss the cut apples with brown sugar, cinnamon and the lemon juice. Set aside. Melt 2 tablespoons of the butter in a large skillet over medium heat. Add the apple mixture and sauté for 10 minutes, stirring occasionally until caramelized. Let the mixture cool while preparing the cake.

Mix the sugar, remaining 2 Tbs. butter (melted), eggs, milk, salt, sugar and Nearly Normal Gluten-Free Flour Mix™ together for 2 – 3 minutes in a mixing bowl or using a food processor. Arrange slightly cooled apples in the bottom of each muffin tin or in the large pan. Pour the batter over the apples and bake for approximately 15 minutes if using large muffin tins, or 25 minutes if using one large pan. After cooking, dust the cakes lightly with Confectioner's sugar and serve immediately.

OLD-FASHIONED RICE PUDDING

This recipe calls for pearl or pudding rice, which is available at most organic or health foods stores. My recipe makes a traditional British form of rice pudding, to which you can add cinnamon, raisins, cranberries, or any other addition you find yummy. It is definitely a feel-good food and makes even a cold rainy day seem a little better.

3 Tbs. short-grain pudding rice
2 ½ cups milk
2 Tbs. light brown sugar
½ tsp. vanilla extract
1 Tbs. butter or margarine
sugar and cinnamon mixture

Preheat oven to 325 F.

Grease or butter a shallow baking dish.

Mix the rice, milk, brown sugar and vanilla extract together in a bowl. Add raisins, cranberries or other additions, if desired. Pour into the greased baking dish and dot the top of the mixture with butter to taste.

Bake for 30 minutes, then stir the skin into the pudding.

Bake for 1 hour more, stirring the skin into the pudding again. Sprinkle sugar and cinnamon mixture on the top, if desired.

Continue to bake for 1 – 2 hours, depending on your oven, removing when the pudding is set through.

Nearly Normal Cooking™ for Gluten-Free Eating

PEANUT BUTTER COOKIES I

These cookies are an easy solution to afternoon peanut butter cravings! The most time-consuming portion of this simple four ingredient recipe is waiting for the sweetened condensed milk to pour out of the can! My husband loves the end result because they are very chewy. Make sure to use real peanut butter, not the "no sugar added" or "natural" kinds; reduced fat varieties are fine to use.

¾ cup smooth or crunchy peanut butter
2 cups Nearly Normal Gluten-Free Flour Mix™
1 14 oz. can sweetened condensed milk (fat free works fine)
1 tsp. vanilla extract

Preheat oven to 375 F.

Beat peanut butter and the can of milk until smooth. Add the Nearly Normal Gluten-Free Flour Mix™ and then the vanilla extract . Mix well and then shape into balls by rolling a teaspoon-sized scoop between the palms of your hands. Roll the balls in a bowl of sugar and place onto an ungreased cookie sheet. Press a criss-crossed design into the tops of the cookies with a fork dipped in sugar. Bake for 10 minutes or until lightly browned.

PEANUT BUTTER COOKIES II

These cookies taste just like the real thing. They're addictive, so be careful!!!

1/3 cup smooth peanut butter
¼ cup sugar
½ cup brown sugar
3 Tbs. shortening, softened (not melted)
¼ cup commercially prepared oil substitute, applesauce or plain yogurt
1 egg, lightly beaten
1 ½ cups Nearly Normal Gluten-Free Flour Mix™
½ tsp. salt
2 Tbs. +/- water

Preheat oven to 350 F.

Mix together all ingredients in the order listed. Add only as much water as needed to hold the dough together without being crumbly.

On an ungreased cookie sheet, place rounded teaspoonfuls of dough. Dip a fork in sugar and press into the tops of each cookie in a criss-cross pattern. Bake for 10 minutes, or until the bottoms of the cookies are slightly browned.

Nearly Normal Cooking™ for Gluten-Free Eating

PEANUT BUTTER
CRISPY RICE TREATS

We all grew up loving these but have been denied even such a simple pleasure unless we make them ourselves using gluten-free cereal. Fortunately, such an option is available and just as delicious. I add peanut butter chips to my recipe for added flavor; straight peanut butter tends to make the treats mushy after they cool. My son likes to decorate with seasonal sugar sprinkles to make the treats more festive.

3 Tbs. margarine or butter
1 package (10 oz., 40 large or 4 cups miniature) marshmallows
6 cups gluten-free crispy rice cereal (do NOT use puffy rice cereal)
½ cup peanut butter chips
colored sprinkles, if desired

Melt margarine on the stovetop over low heat and add the marshmallows, stirring constantly until melted. Remove from heat and gradually add the cereal into the marshmallow mixture. Add the peanut butter chips before the mixture hardens, then pour into a greased 9 x 13 pan. Use a rubber spatula or a small square of waxed paper that has been sprayed with non-stick cooking spray to pat the mixture into the pan and make it smooth. Sprinkle with colored sugar and allow to cool before cutting.

*BAKING TIP: Pre-measure the marshmallows and cereal and set aside before beginning the recipe. Work quickly so that the mixture does not set up before you have mixed all the ingredients!

PECAN CRANBERRY TASSIES

This recipe comes to me from a Canadian friend who is very creative with her gluten-free kitchen. Like me, her barometer for success is her non-celiac husband. He apparently puts in routine requests for these unbelievably tasty little treats! They are indeed worth the effort and can be frozen for several days before serving.

Dough:
2 sticks (1 cup) of unsalted butter, softened
6 oz. cream cheese
2 cups of Nearly Normal Gluten-Free Flour Mix™

Filling:
3 large eggs, slightly beaten
1 ¾ cups packed brown sugar
3 Tbs. unsalted butter, melted
¾ tsp. vanilla extract
¾ cup dried cranberries
¼ tsp. salt
1 cup pecans, coarsely chopped

Confectioner's sugar

To make the dough, beat the butter and cream cheese with mixer on medium speed until well mixed. Add in the Nearly Normal Gluten-Free Flour Mix™ until just blended. Shape dough into a 1 in. thick disk, wrap and refrigerate at least 30 minutes until firm.

Preheat oven to 375 F.

Have an ungreased mini muffin pan ready. Divide dough into quarters and roll each portion into a 6 inch long log. Cut 1 log into 12 equal pieces. With hands dusted with cornstarch, flatten each piece to a 3 inch round and fit into a muffin cup (dough should extend above the cup slightly.)

Beat first 6 "Filling" ingredients until well mixed. Spoon 2 teaspoons full into each muffin cup and top with pecans. Bake 20 minutes or until pastry is brown and filling is set. Cool briefly in pan, then carefully remove cups, loosening them with the tip of a knife if needed. Place on a wire rack to cool. Repeat with remaining dough. Dust tassies with Confectioner's sugar.

Nearly Normal Cooking™ for Gluten-Free Eating

PINEAPPLE UPSIDE-DOWN CAKE

This cake is particularly good with fresh pineapple, but even canned pineapple rings work well to make this moist and flavorful cake.

<u>Cake:</u>
1 ⅓ cup Nearly Normal Gluten-Free Flour Mix™
3 tsp. baking powder
dash of salt
½ tsp. guar gum
⅔ cup sugar
1 egg
3 Tbs. oil or vanilla yogurt
½ tsp. baking soda
¾ milk

<u>Topping:</u>
½ cup brown sugar
6 sliced pineapple rings
1 small jar of maraschino cherries (optional)

Preheat oven to 350 F.

In a large bowl, combine all ingredients but milk; add milk by slowly mixing in until all lumps are removed.

Set aside.

Sprinkle brown sugar on the bottom of a greased round cake pan. Place rings of pineapple on top of brown sugar in a circular pattern.

Pour batter on top of the pineapple and cover with foil. Bake for 25 minutes, then remove foil and cook another 15 – 20 minutes until a cake tester inserted in the middle of the cake tests clean. Allow to cool for 10 minutes before inverting cake pan onto serving plate.

PUMPKIN CHEESECAKE

Pumpkin + cheesecake = delicious!

Crust:
1 ¼ cup finely crushed gluten-free graham crackers (see pg. 122), rice bran crackers
     or gingersnaps
½ cup finely chopped pecans
2 Tbs. melted butter

Filling:
2/3 cup vanilla yogurt
2 (8 oz.) pkgs. light cream cheese, softened
1 ¾ cups canned pumpkin
2 eggs, lightly beaten
½ cup sugar
½ cup brown sugar
1 ½ cups evaporated milk
1 Tbs. pumpkin pie spice
dash of salt
1 tsp. vanilla extract

Preheat oven to 350 F.

Combine graham cracker crumbs, pecans and butter in a bowl and mix well. Firmly press mixture into the bottom of a greased 9-inch spring form pan or pie plate. Chill the pan in the freezer while preparing the filling.

Mix yogurt and cream cheese until creamy. Add the remaining filling ingredients and beat until creamy. Pour filling into crust and bake for 2 hours, or until the middle only slightly jiggles when tapped.

Cool on a baking rack and then in the refrigerator for at least 4 hours before serving. If desired, garnish with whipped topping and a sprinkle of cinnamon.

PUMPKIN PIE

Use Grandma's Perfect Pie Crust recipe on page 124 , and your guests will never know they're indulging in anything but traditional holiday fare!

15 – oz. can of pumpkin
14 – oz. can of sweetened condensed milk
2 eggs
4 tsp. ground cinnamon
2 tsp. ground ginger
2 tsp. ground nutmeg
½ tsp. salt

Preheat oven to 425 F.

Whisk all ingredients until smooth. Pour into unbaked pie crust and sprinkle with cinnamon. Bake for 15 minutes with pie crust edges covered with foil or commercial crust covers. Reduce heat to 350 F and continue baking for 35 – 40 minutes, or until a knife inserted into the center comes out clean. You may remove the covering from the pie crust with about 15 minutes left. Cool and refrigerate if there are any leftovers!

RUM CAKE

Ever a favorite in my household at holiday time, I feared I would never again be able to partake of this delicious and festive treat. I've fortunately found a gluten-free solution and am willing to share! This is one of those recipes that my finicky husband tastes every year and says, "this is gluten-free? Wow!"

2 2/3 cup Nearly Normal Gluten-Free Flour Mix™
1 Tbs. plus 2 tsp. baking powder
½ tsp. guar gum
1 cup sugar
2 tsp. vanilla extract
dash of salt

(OR use a commercial gluten-free yellow cake mix that makes two 8-inch round cakes) then add the following ingredients:

1 package gluten-free vanilla instant pudding dry mix (3.4 oz.)
4 eggs
½ cup light rum
½ cup oil
1 cup chopped pecans

Preheat oven to 325 F.

Add and beat all ingredients, except nuts, for 2 minutes on medium speed. Grease and "flour" a bunt pan with cornstarch. Sprinkle with 1 cup chopped pecans. Pour batter on top of the nuts and bake for 50 minutes.

Topping:
1 cup sugar
¼ cup light rum
¼ cup water

Boil all for 5 minutes, then pour over the hot cake while still in the pan. Let stand for 30 minutes, then flip the cake onto a plate and enjoy!

STREUSEL

This dessert is great for a breakfast dish or a dessert with ice cream on top!

Pastry:
1 egg
½ cup sour cream
½ tsp. apple cider vinegar
2 Tbs. shortening
2 Tbs. honey
2 Tbs. sugar
1 tsp. vanilla extract
1 Tbs. yeast
1 cup Nearly Normal Gluten-Free Flour Mix™
½ tsp. baking soda
1 tsp. baking powder
dash of salt

Preheat oven to 350 F.

Mix all streusel ingredients until the lumps are removed. Arrange the wet dough in the bottom of a 9 x 13 baking dish with cornstarch dusted or wet fingers.

Filling:
¼ cup milk
½ cup shortening
¾ cup sugar
1 cup Nearly Normal Gluten-Free Flour Mix™
2 tsp. baking powder
dash of salt
1 tsp. cinnamon

Mix all ingredients until a crumbly mixture is achieved. Sprinkle or spread over the streusel pastry and bake 25 minutes or until the top is lightly browned and a cake tester or toothpick inserted into the center of the dish is clean.

TOFU PUMPKIN CHEESECAKE

I suggest adding pumpkin purée to this recipe because it's so delicious, but you can also leave out the pumpkin and spices and enjoy this healthy (?!) cheesecake in its purest form.

12 oz. package of extra firm tofu
1 ¼ cup sugar
2 (8 oz.) pkgs. light cream cheese, at room temperature
1 tsp. cornstarch
1 ⅓ cups pumpkin purée
1 Tbs. vanilla extract
2 tsp. cinnamon
¼ tsp. ground allspice
¼ tsp. ground cloves
6 egg whites
1 large bag of gluten-free gingersnaps (see pg. 121) or graham-like crackers (pg. 122)

Preheat oven to 350 F.

Lightly grease a springform pan and set aside. Crumble enough gingersnaps to cover the bottom of the pan in a ¼ inch crust. You can do this in a food processor, blender or the old fashioned way — by placing the cookies in a large ziptop bag and running a rolling pin over the cookies until they reach the desired consistency. Sprinkle the crumbs over the bottom of the pan.

Purée the tofu in a blender or food processor until smooth. Add sugar and the cream cheese blocks and blend. Add the pumpkin and spices plus the cornstarch and blend until smooth. Finally, add the egg whites and blend just until it is thoroughly mixed. Pour the mixture into the pan and bake for 1 hour or until the cheesecake is puffy and the center is nearly set. Cool the cake on a wire rack. Run a butter knife or stiff rubber spatula around the sides to loosen the cake when cooled.

YELLOW CAKE

This cake works nicely for a layered birthday cake or sheet cake for a neighborhood picnic.

2 2/3 cups Nearly Normal Gluten-Free Flour Mix™
1 Tbs. plus 2 tsp. baking powder
1 tsp. salt
½ tsp. guar gum
1 cup sugar
2 eggs
¼ cup oil or vanilla yogurt
2 tsp. vanilla extract
2 cups milk

Preheat oven to 350 F.

Combine all ingredients except milk. Mix until all lumps are removed. Slowly add the milk until mixed thoroughly, but do not overmix. Pour into a greased 9 x 13 pan or two greased and "floured" with cornstarch round cake pans. Bake for 25 minutes or until a cake tester inserted into the middle of the pan(s) tests clean.

Cool on wire rack and frost with your favorite icing.

YOGURT CORN CAKE

This is a nice summer option with fresh fruit.

1 cup cornmeal
1 cup Nearly Normal Gluten-Free Flour Mix™
2 tsp. baking powder
½ tsp. baking soda
½ tsp. salt
½ cup sugar + 2 Tbs. sugar to sprinkle on berries
2 cups vanilla yogurt
1 egg
⅓ cup vegetable oil
1 cup sliced strawberries
1 cup blueberries (or other berry)
¼ cup orange juice

Preheat oven to 400 F.

Combine the cornmeal, Nearly Normal Gluten-Free Flour Mix™, baking powder, baking soda, salt and ½ cup sugar in a bowl. Add only 1 cup of the yogurt, the beaten egg and oil. Mix just until blended. Pour batter into a greased 9-inch round pan and bake for 25 – 30 minutes, or until firm to the touch and golden in color. Cool slightly before cutting. Meanwhile, mix the berries with 2 tsp. sugar and juice. Let the berries stand for 15 minutes. Serve sliced cake with ¼ cup berry mixture and a dollop of yogurt.

ZUCCHINI BROWNIES

Don't be put off by the name of these delicious treats! This recipe came to me from my grandmother, who first gave me the idea of slipping green vegetables into my unsuspecting kids' food! No child (or picky adult, for that matter!) will ever suspect that these moist, nutty cake-like brownies have anything good for you inside!

2 eggs
½ cup oil
¼ cup vanilla yogurt
1 cup sugar
1 cup Nearly Normal Gluten-Free Flour Mix™
1 tsp. baking soda
1 tsp. cinnamon
½ tsp. salt
2 Tbs. cocoa
1 tsp. vanilla extract
1 ½ cups grated zucchini
½ cup chopped nuts

Preheat the oven to 350 F.

Beat together the first four ingredients then add the remaining ingredients until the batter is thoroughly mixed. Spread batter into a greased 8 x 8 baking pan, or in individual ramekins. Bake for 25 – 40 minutes, depending on the size of the pans. Remove from the oven when the batter is no longer shiny and wiggly and when a cake tester inserted into the center of the brownies comes out nearly clean.

RECIPE INDEX

Nearly Normal Cooking™ for Gluten-Free Eating

Desserts 99

Nearly Normal Cooking™ for Gluten-Free Eating

SELECTED INGREDIENT INDEX

Nearly Normal Cooking™ for Gluten-Free Eating

EQUIVALENT MEASUREMENTS

Dry

3 teaspoons	=	1 Tablespoon
2 Tablespoons	=	⅛ cup
4 Tablespoons	=	¼ cup
5 Tablespoons + 1 teaspoon	=	⅓ cup
8 Tablespoons	=	½ cup
10 Tablespoons + 2 teaspoons	=	⅔ cup
12 Tablespoons	=	¾ cup
16 Tablespoons	=	1 cup

Liquid

2 Tablespoons	=	1 ounce
1 cup	=	8 ounces
2 cups	=	1 pint or 16 ounces
4 cups	=	1 quart
4 quarts	=	1 gallon

Nearly Normal Cooking™ for Gluten-Free Eating